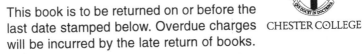

Dedicated to:

My inspiration, my boys, Bob, Matthew and Simon

Developing
Decision Makers

An
empowerment approach
to coaching

Lynn Kidman

With guest authors Rod Thorpe, Robyn Jones and Craig Lewis

Innovative
PRINT COMMUNICATIONS LTD

First Published in 2001
by
Innovative Print Communications Ltd
P.O. Box 31 259
Christchurch
New Zealand
website: www.ipcltd.com
email: info@ipcltd.com

ISBN : 0-473-07587-3

Editor: Tanya Tremewan

Printer: Wyatt and Wilson Printers Ltd.

Cover design: Jay James, Slide Design

Table of Contents

Preface

Developing Decision Makers: An Empowerment Approach to Coaching offers insight into an approach that coaches can use to create an optimal learning environment for their athletes. When coaches give power to athletes, allowing them to make better decisions and enhancing their long-term learning, athletes are motivated to participate to the best of their ability.

One of our major roles in coaching is to enable athletes to learn. In an empowerment approach, athletes take ownership of their learning, thus increasing their opportunities and strengthening their abilities to retain important skills and ideas. This learning develops athletes' ability to make informed decisions during competitions, an important element in successful performance at any sporting level.

Developing Decision Makers begins by defining empowerment as a coaching approach. The first chapter introduces empowerment, compares it to traditional approaches and discusses why coaches should consider using it. The first chapter also discusses how to develop empowerment coaching philosophies. In this regard, it introduces Wayne Smith (ex-Crusaders coach, current All Blacks coach), who was observed and interviewed for this publication as a model of a coach using an empowerment approach successfully. Later chapters (especially Chapter Three, a dedicated case study) return to Wayne Smith's ideas expressed in his own words, as his story illustrates how the approach works and may inspire other coaches to develop an empowering style.

In Chapter Two, through excerpts from a written interview, Rod Thorpe from Loughborough University describes Teaching Games for Understanding (Game Sense), a major strategy in empowerment. Moving away from the use of traditional drills that are irrelevant to the actual sport, the key factor of Game Sense is the game. Coaches design their training sessions to make the drills more game-like so that athletes learn about tactics and skills. Wayne Smith and the developing coaches interviewed for this book use the Game Sense approach extensively.

The stories of two developing junior coaches (i.e. coaches who are just starting and using the approach with their teams) are presented in Chapter Four. Hugh Galvan and Paul McKay provide insight into the benefits and pitfalls they have encountered in learning about and developing an empowerment approach. Included too are comments that the players in their team made in written evaluations, which reinforce the value of empowerment as a coaching tool, in interesting ways.

In Chapter Five, Robyn Jones, a university lecturer and coach, discusses the benefits, potential pitfalls and other issues that coaches should consider when implementing the approach. His purpose is to illustrate how coaches can implement an empowerment approach in a range of situations. He emphasises the importance of developing an approach appropriate to the level of the athletes (i.e. children or élite).

Two athletes (Daryl Gibson and Anna Veronese) provide their perceptions of the empowerment approach in Chapter Six. They describe how they reacted initially, how the approach contributes to their development and how it affects their team. They also discuss any misgivings that they or other team members may have had about the approach.

Craig Lewis, Director of Sportlife, discusses the athlete as a person (not just a sport jock) in Chapter Seven. Craig has developed Sportlife, a concept and programme being scrutinised by many professional teams. He suggests how coaches can help athletes to balance their life and in so doing enhance their ability to contribute to their sport. Consistent with an empowerment philosophy, he takes a holistic, humanistic perspective of the athlete.

One of the key components to empowerment, including the strategy of Game Sense, is that coaches ask questions that encourage athlete self-awareness and learning about tactics and skills. Chapter Eight gives practical guidelines for planning and asking meaningful questions. The technique of questioning is addressed as well as the art of asking meaningful questions.

As most coaches work with children, Chapter Nine concentrates on sport and children, our future athletes. Issues discussed relate to why children participate in sport, the value of and concerns about competition, and strategies to provide child athletes with a positive sporting experience so that they continue to participate in sport. The influence of significant others (such as parents) is also considered.

Lastly, Chapter Ten pulls together the many different ideas raised in the book, so that coaches can put empowerment into practice. Part of implementation is self-reflective analysis, a tool that coaches can use to monitor their ongoing coaching. The purpose of the chapter, building on the momentum of the chapters before it, is to encourage coaches to start to use empowerment, reflect on how they use it and continue to improve their approach.

Acknowledgements

There are many people I would like to thank for their various contributions to *Developing Decision Makers*. This book would have been impossible without the constant critical discussion with the students in the Bachelor of Sport Coaching degree at Christchurch College of Education. I thank them for their inquisitive minds and the challenges that enable coaches to be the best they can be.

I would like to express a special thanks to Wayne Smith, who selflessly gave his advice and expertise about his own coaching and ways of thinking. It is great to have someone to return us to the real values that sport has to offer.

I would also like to thank Rod Thorpe who inspired me in his workshops and also gives selflessly to the cause of educating sport coaches.

Thank you to Robyn Jones and Craig Lewis, who offered their sound advice to coaches in their endless pursuit of developing great coaches.

Thanks to Hugh Galvan and Paul McKay, humble coaches who see their important role as coach educators. It was great to see them both trial the empowerment approach with their teams and achieve such success. It must be worth it, coaches!! Also to Hugh who provided advice on what the coaches might want to hear and listened to my ranting and raving about what to title the book. Hugh constantly challenged and helped me to learn about this empowerment approach to coaching.

To Daryl Gibson and Anna Veronese, who drew on their experience of their participation and the coaches they have had, thanks for being honest and enlightening. As coaches, we need to listen to athletes better.

To Ross Tasker, who spent many hours reading and providing feedback to chapter drafts, thank you for your time and energy.

Of course, there is the editor of the book, Tanya Tremewan, who was amazing in her ability to develop the text to make it readable. Thanks Tanya for having such a great talent. You make it seem so easy.

Chapter One

Questions provide the key to un-
locking our unlimited potential.

—Anthony Robbins

What is Empowerment?

Coaching is a complex process. Coaches are responsible for enabling athletes to learn. Like other learners, athletes develop understanding when they are involved in solving problems for themselves, thus enhancing their learning (Butler, 1997). Important tools in the learning process are to develop new ideas, knowledge and the ability to make decisions. If experts merely present knowledge (sometimes quite forcefully) to those who are 'nonexpert' and make decisions for them, the athletes become disempowered. In other words, if athletes' needs do not influence their learning experiences, learning is minimal. The knowledge, understanding, skill and decision-making ability that athletes learn and apply can make the difference between performance success and failure.

When coaches use an empowering style of coaching, athletes gain and take ownership of knowledge, development and decision making that will help them to maximise their performance. An empowerment approach provides athletes with a chance to be part of the vision and values of sports teams.

The word *empowerment* has many meanings. For this chapter, after an outline of the current practice of coaches, empowerment is defined and discussed in the sporting context. An empowerment approach to coaching emphasises an athlete-centred approach rather than a traditional prescriptive (or autocratic) style of coaching. The athlete-centred approach promotes a sense of belonging, as well as giving athletes a role in decision making and a shared approach to learning. Finally in this chapter, a practical application of empowerment is offered through a discussion of how to create an empowering philosophy.

Current Coaching Practices

To maximise athlete performance, coaches, like leaders of formal organisations, combine the power of their position with a particular leadership style. Although coaching today encompasses a wide variety of approaches, the traditional leadership style has given coaches a licence to 'exploit' their power by taking the choice and control away from the athlete. When a coach takes total control and athletes have basically no say, the approach is called *prescriptive* or autocratic. Sometimes this style has been described, mistakenly, as an important element in coaching success.

A prescriptive coach endeavours to control athlete behaviour not only throughout training and competition, but also beyond the sport setting. A prescriptive coach tends to coach athletes as if they are on a factory assembly line. Athletes of prescriptive coaches are often 'hooked' into a limited form of learning that emphasises memorising rather than understanding or solving problems. This limited approach encourages athletes to be robotic in their actions and thinking. They do not experience themselves as having an active role in contributing to or being a part of their learning.

In the professional era, the performance objectives of many coaches depend on winning. The expectation is that coaches may be held accountable for many uncertainties beyond the coaches' control (e.g. injuries, exceptional play by the opposition, poor officiating, the weather). In reacting to this pressure on themselves, coaches tend to give athletes extraordinarily gruelling training sessions that demand more than the athletes can give; sometimes they use dehumanising practices to enforce their control (Pratt & Eitzen, 1989). Unfortunately, for coaches like these, the pressure in this professional 'must-win' environment becomes so great that coaches 'take over' in an attempt to ensure their athletes are winning. The directions become coach-centred, rather than mutual between the athletes and the coach.

This disempowering form of coach control actually contradicts why many athletes are participating in sport. It can have detrimental effects on the athletes who are controlled. The coach can also suffer when the athletes reject such control. In these controlling situations the benefits of winning can be limited. If a team is winning, the athletes smile, but if a team loses or tires of being bossed around, generally the team environment deteriorates.

If athletes truly learn and take ownership of the direction of the team or competition, there is a better chance that success will result. Success for athletes is rarely winning; it is usually focused on achieving their goals. A prescriptive coach mistakenly assumes that athletes are there to win and seldom determines why athletes participate in sport. Conversely, as part of an empowering approach, one of the coach's first roles is to determine the reasons why each athlete is participating, and to establish a vision and direction for the season that both the athletes and the coach own.

As the above discussion indicates, the opposite of empowerment is *disempowerment*. The traditional prescriptive approach disempowers athletes, yet it is still evident in many sports. With a prescriptive style, reading the game is largely a prescription from the coach (like playing a chess game). Yet such a game can be a learning experience that encourages athletes to understand the game and choose options based on informed decisions. The need for such an approach is obvious in many sports throughout the world (e.g. rugby, rugby league, soccer, athletics) where there are often long periods when the coach is not directly involved in making decisions on the field and communication with the athletes is limited. More broadly, informed decisions by athletes are essential to performance success in every sport, as in every sport it is the athlete who competes, not the coach.

When coaching in tactics and skills at training sessions, prescriptive coaches traditionally tend to give athletes specific directions on what to 'fix' or the exact moves to perform. In some cases, coaches believe that unless they are seen to be telling athletes what to do and how to do it, they are not doing their job properly. Some coaches believe that they are expected to win and that successful coaches are (and should be) hard-nosed and discipline-oriented. Others view their role as one of promoting enjoyment and personal development (supportive, empowering coaches).

Much of the research suggests that no matter what coaching style is used, athletes respond better to supportive coaches rather than punitive coaches (Smoll & Smith, 1989). Ironically, coaches who follow the prescriptive approach often express concerns related to low athlete productivity, poor performance quality and lack of motivation and commitment by athletes (Usher, 1997). In contrast, athletes with supportive coaches show greater intrinsic motivation, enjoy participating and competing in sport, make informed decisions more rapidly in the ever-changing game and demonstrate that trust is mutual (player–player, player–coach, coach–player, coach–coach).

Although a prescriptive approach is necessary in some instances, traditional coaches can abuse their influence. Coaches are considered the 'power' within a team and this status leads to an unquestioned acceptance of a coach's leadership style among athletes and significant others (parents, administrators, public). In this environment coaches do not and cannot listen to their athletes, as they believe that if they listen they will be perceived as losing their 'power'. Such an environment ensures that coaches do what they want regardless of the personal and collective needs of the athletes.

Such coaches make many assumptions about athletes. For example, they may assume that because athletes are participating, they want to be champions and they will pay the price required to achieve this end. Often teams with this style of coaching have short-term success at the beginning of the season, but start floundering later in the season when they are not able to make decisions.

A very different pattern may be evident with teams coached on empowerment principles. Wayne Smith (All Blacks coach) agrees that if teams can keep their cool, react to what they see, talk and guts it out and be relentless, they can get to the top every time. Wayne suggests that teams with empowering approaches often tend to be:

> middling to fair earlier, but as athletes are developing a team culture, developing a way of learning, they are actually going to be more knowledgeable and understand the game better as the season progresses.

In the changing world of sport, the 'prescriptive' approach has been rightly challenged. This book argues that a prescriptive coaching approach takes success away from the athlete and emphasises the coach's total domination of his or her sporting teams (and/or individual athletes). The information here supports and encourages empowerment as a coaching approach. An empowerment style of coaching is one of the most innovative and effective approaches to coaching, enabling athletes to succeed in and enjoy their sporting participation. Through it, athletes can create something significant and perhaps different from current practices within their sport. Athletes and teams can lead the way by using innovative ideas to make the game or competition more exciting. In the empowering process coaches and athletes work for similar purposes within a motivating environment. An empowerment approach helps to motivate athletes and gives them a sense of satisfaction in being part of a common vision, so the 'team' can grow in the same direction.

What is this Empowerment?

The term empowerment comes from sociology theory. Although used in a variety of ways, at a general level it may be thought of as a process by which people gain more control over decisions that affect their lives. It counteracts the process whereby dominant power groups tend to 'co-opt, or appropriate, new and emerging ideologies ...' (Eskes, Duncan & Miller, 1998, p. 320). With empowerment the individual has a voice.

Thus an empowered athlete has some choice and control over what happens in his or her sporting life, through training and in general lifestyle. The athletes and team have choice and control because the 'power' is given to them (Arai, 1997). They have the authority and are able to actively engage fully in shaping and defining their own direction (Freysinger & Bedini, 1994). For coaching, an important implication of empowerment is that athletes take ownership of their own learning and direction.

Some of the main advantages to using empowerment in coaching are that athletes are motivated to learn and they have a greater understanding and retention of both tactics and skills (psychological, emotional and physical) that are so important to success in sport. In sport, a coach who empowers his or her athletes facilitates their learning but does not control it. Athletes are required to be self-sufficient in their performance, decision making and option taking while participating in their respective sports; an empowering approach encourages athletes to become self-aware and self-sufficient. Such an approach allows athletes to make informed decisions and emphasises individual growth and change.

Many coaches practise coaching without really understanding the process. Coaching is a complex mix of behaviours, characteristics, knowledge and effectiveness, yet coaches often have not had or taken the opportunity to be trained. The variety of styles that coaches use are often modelled on coaching styles that were practised when they were athletes. Although there is no 'ideal' model of coaching, alternatives to these traditional, disempowering coaching styles must be encouraged to increase athletes' understanding of their sport and of life more generally. An effective coaching style will enable athletes to be open to opportunities for decision making.

In the employment world, industrial productivity is related to job satisfaction. This link can be applied to sport, in that a team is more productive if they enjoy what they do. This idea is the basis to an empowerment approach, which focuses on the individual and his or her growth in both sport and life. Empowerment coaching builds a committed partnership between the athlete/team and the coach. In this partnership, the coach acts as a facilitator or catalyst for athletes' optimal performance. Goals are mutual and teamwork is enhanced, therefore success results. An empowering coach helps athletes learn and enables them to understand how to exceed their current limits. The coach nurtures involvement and autonomy in the athletes' learning (Usher, 1997).

A number of successful coaches (e.g. Wayne Smith, All Blacks coach; Rick Charlesworth, Australian women's hockey coach) base their style on an empowerment approach that encourages athletes to become self-aware of skill execution and tactical play. Their approach is concerned with questioning (see Chapter Eight) rather than prescription (Hadfield, 1994; Kidman, 1996). When coaches question athletes and encourage them to ask questions, they enable the athletes to take ownership of their learning and athletic environment. The coach who uses an empowering style divests himself or herself of power, however gradually, and hands it to the athletes (Kidman, Hadfield & Chu, 2000).

The empowering approach does not suggest that the coach should give full responsibility to athletes. Rather, coaches should exercise their leadership by guiding athletes towards decision making and allowing them to take their own responsibility for sport participation. Clearly in some situations, with some athletes, coaches need to be more prescriptive, but the aim should always be to encourage self-reliance through decision making.

Arai (1997) suggested that in becoming empowered, individuals move through several stages in this order:

1. becoming self-aware

2. connecting and learning

3. taking action

4. contributing to their own learning.

In the first stage, coaches facilitate athletes' awareness level. To determine if they are empowered, athletes should assess themselves and begin to increase their self-awareness. They also need to identify whether they feel they belong to the group or whether they feel alienated, so they can determine their role within the team. It is important for athletes to establish how committed they feel and how important this sport is to their life. Self-aware athletes also understand why they make certain moves and react in certain ways, why they perform the way they do and their own body movement. A coach can help athletes to improve their self-awareness by asking meaningful questions. For example, asking 'Why did you move there?', 'What were you doing when you contacted the ball?' or 'How do you think you can get that pass away quicker?' will help athletes to focus their thoughts on what they are doing.

In stage 2 athletes determine their role in learning. To gain an understanding of their own responsibility for learning, athletes must first change their view of what learning is. One of the initial steps is for them to understand that they need to be a part of their own learning. A coach's role is to provide support, to be a mentor and act as an information source so that athletes can begin to expand on their choices and opportunities.

In stage 3 athletes apply the new information about themselves and learning, to take action in the empowering process. They engage in new activities and begin to become decision makers through expressing their own ideas. In this stage, athletes act in empowered ways: they ask questions, they answer coaches' questions, they participate with awareness of their own performance. At this stage they begin to become part of the learning process rather than an observer. The coach's role here is to encourage and support the athletes' ideas and sense of self-expression.

In stage 4 athletes contribute to their own learning by processing their thinking and gaining an understanding that enhances their ability to solve problems and make decisions. They contribute to the vision and goals of the team and of themselves, ask and answer questions and decide on their own fate. Athletes have a sense of belonging and acceptance from the coach and other athletes. A coach's role is to encourage the growth of this individual and of the team collectively. The role emphasises support and facilitation—and only if needed.

In summary, empowered athletes:

- understand responsibility in the sense that they are accountable, able and willing to act, and accept the consequences of that action;

- develop a sense of self-efficacy or ability to control results produced by their skill and effort;

- understand that power comes from within, not from without;

 - understand that power is an agreement between two people based on mutual trust;

- are more coachable because they let go of the need to be controlled;

- are highly committed to achieving levels of excellence;

- are willing to engage totally in what they believe (Usher, 1997, p. 11).

Creating an Empowering Philosophy

It is useful for all coaches to formulate a coaching philosophy or personal statement about the values and beliefs important to their understanding of sport and life. This philosophy provides the foundation that directs the way athletes are coached (Kidman & Hanrahan, 1997). It is important for coaches to go through this process of thinking about why they are coaching, then write it down and analyse it. It can feel quite threatening to put your own philosophy down on paper, but thinking through your philosophy is an enlightening process.

As coaches learn, they tend to think through their philosophy again and change their attitudes and values in accordance with individual needs. Because these changes will affect a coaching philosophy, reviewing the philosophy regularly and altering it to fit with each coach's experience are important features of the process.

The value systems that underpin a coach's approach are crucial in determining the needs of both coaches and athletes. As the basis of the coach's knowledge, these values will be important to guide any of the coach's actions. In addition, it is the coach's responsibility to communicate this philosophy to athletes so that they are encouraged to achieve their goals. Every sport setting needs a philosophical base so that the team or individual can develop and learn according to a consistent, coherent way of thinking.

Under an empowering philosophy, part of a coach's facilitation role is to define the nature of these guidelines and to follow the empowering philosophy in his or her approach to coaching. As mentioned above, one goal of empowerment is to establish mutual visions, whereby coaches facilitate the process of setting priorities for the good of the team and/or athletes. Developing an empowering philosophy where athletes are encouraged to become self-aware and self-reliant in decision making provides a foundation that contributes to the holistic development of individual athletes. The whole season should be built on the belief system that athletes and coaches have created mutually.

An empowering philosophy is athlete-centred. For a philosophy to be empowering, the coach needs to consider what empowerment means to him or her and how to ensure that true empowerment exists for the athletes.

The holistic development of the athlete is central to the success of empowerment as a coaching approach. The athletes are the central focus of any team and determine the success or failure of the season. The quality experience that the athletes gain from a season will depend on the value systems, principles and beliefs of both the coach and athletes. Successful coach Wayne Smith describes the holistic, athlete-centred approach he incorporates in his sound empowering philosophy, where his role is:

> ... to create an environment so that the players feel comfortable in making decisions. In this way, they can cope with responsibilities and they can take ownership of their learning. Players should own the team culture. They should set their own expectations, establish the team protocols, ... create the vision and the values. We (as coaches) guide them and facilitate them, but it is their total 'buy in' (collectively) that we are after. It's their programme, their campaign. So, my philosophy is to create empowered players and, to have ... a holistic type approach so that the players are not just sport jocks, not just training for rugby, but have outside interests. I believe coaching is all about trying to develop better people, not just better players and it's important to enjoy the whole experience.

A philosophy is based on ideas formed from experiences. These experiences stem from influential teachers, coaches or mentors who have had a positive or negative effect on aspects of your life. For example, many people will have analysed another coach's approach and concluded, 'I will never be like that because she destroys the athletes. She scared many of the kids away.' Conversely, many will have been coached under or observed many positive philosophies that they can drawn on in creating their own philosophy.

In developing a personal coaching philosophy:

· ask why a particular teacher/coach had such a meaningful impact on you and what happened;

· determine how or whether those experiences may direct personal coaching actions;

· develop opinion(s) based on the knowledge that you have gathered over the years;

· determine any hopes for the future.

Success vs Winning

To many people, success is measured by how many games or competitions are won or lost. Many coaches' jobs depend on how many matches have been won or lost. Success, however, is not just about winning. Striving to win is more important. Wayne Smith has suggested that his most successful season was his first year of coaching the Canterbury Crusaders:

> It was a brilliant year, the best year of rugby I'd ever had in my life, either playing or coaching. We didn't even make the semi-finals, but we built a lot of self-esteem. We had players who, in interviews at the start of the season, said they didn't feel they should be on the same field as Auckland. Just getting them to the point where they could hold their heads high, where they knew they understood the game better than most players around the country was satisfying. We were starting to do something special and we knew it. It was a process of building self-confidence and belief. It was very rewarding and enjoyable.

Winning is a major factor in sports participation but success is more important. An athlete can win without performing well or can lose even though the performance has been outstanding. Success is a measure of how well the athletes are participating, how well they are achieving both personal and team goals. Winning is where you compare yourself to others. Success is self-measured, based on individual performance and contribution.

Many coaches speak about winning and success as if they have the same meaning. However, winning must be defined within the culture of the team. For example, Wayne Smith's definition of winning is:

> ... what you want it to be really. Winning may be (with a poor team), moving them up to a reasonable position on the ladder. It might be walking into the changing room and seeing smiles on their faces. Winning for me is seeing people enjoying what they're doing, giving it all they have, players to the best of

their ability, but playing because they love the game, not just because they are paid to.

There are many success stories about famous coaches but how many coaches have ensured the success of all their athletes? The attitude of 'win at all costs' is prevalent in many societies, including ours, but what is the cost? How many athletes have been turned away from sport because of their coach's insistence on winning (as in scoring the most points)? In Australia, it has been suggested that the five most common reasons for dropping out of sport are related to the coach (Robertson, 1992).

We rarely hear news about a successful coach who provided a great training environment and encouraged athletes to do their best. The media rarely portray a successful coach as an educator. Nevertheless, one of the biggest jobs in coaching is to educate athletes, preparing them physically, psychologically and socially. Knowing how your athletes tick and drawing out their athletic capabilities are measures of success. Because coaching is a people-oriented job, coaches must know how to facilitate the coaching environment to bring out the best in their athletes and they need to be committed to the individuals with whom they are working. In addition, sport is only part of athletes' lives, not their entire lives, so another measure of success may be whether each athlete continues to participate in sport, either with the same coach or with someone else.

Athletes have different ideas about why they are participating in sport, including different desires, interests, involvement and commitments. Sport offers a setting where athletes can gain a sense of competence, achievement and recognition. Thus taking athletes to the Olympics or coaching an élite professional team is not what makes a coach important. Rather, an important coach is one who introduces individuals to sport and provides them with confidence, success and recognition, so that the athletes want to continue in sport. A coach can make the athletic experience positive or negative. If a coach is dedicated to the pursuit of excellence—that is, excellence for the individual athlete—he or she can offer a profound, enjoyable, positive and successful experience for athletes. Our athletes deserve good coaches, dedicated to athletes' betterment and to the development of confident, motivated, successful and happy people. This dedication is embedded in values and principles of an empowering philosophy.

Coaches are constantly in a predicament as to whether to do what people say, or to do what they believe. As winning is so important to society and the media, it is worthwhile for coaches to consider their philosophy in developing athletes. Is it more important to bow to the media or to keep your own self-esteem? Does the media need to continue to influence our humanist approaches by constantly reporting win/loss records? With the power to make or break an athlete, the coach must be able to say that an athlete achieved success by achieving self-reliance and self-awareness. Ultimately, although a coach's job is never complete, if a coach empowers athletes, he or she should be all but redundant. To ensure true success, coaches need to strive for the self-sufficiency and self-fulfilment of the athlete.

References

Arai, S.M. (1997). Empowerment: from the theoretical to the personal, *Journal of Leisurability, 24*(1), 3–11.

Butler, J. (1997). How would Socrates teach games? A constructivist approach, *Journal of Physical Education, 68*(8), 42–47.

Eskes, T.B., Duncan, M.C., & Miller, E.M. (1998). The discourse of empowerment: Foucault, Marcuse and the women's fitness texts, *Journal of Sport and Social Issues, 23*(3), 317–344.

Freysinger, V., & Bedini, L.A. (1994). Teaching for empowerment, *Schole: A Journal of Leisure Studies and Recreational Education, 9,* 1–11.

Hadfield, D.C. (1994). The query theory: a sports coaching model for the 90's, *The New Zealand Coach, 3*(4), 16–20.

Kidman, L. (1996). A teaching technique for effective coaching: questioning, *The New Zealand Coach, 5*(1), 14–17.

Kidman, L, Hadfield, D., & Chu, M. (2000). The coach and the sporting experience. In C. Collins, *Sport in New Zealand Society,* pp. 273–286. Palmerston North: Dunmore.

Kidman, L., & Hanrahan, S.J. (1997). *The Coaching Process: A Practical Guide to Improving Your Effectiveness.* Palmerston North: Dunmore.

Pratt, S. R., & Eitzen, D.S. (1989). Contrasting leadership styles and organisational effectiveness: the case of athletic teams, *Social Science Quarterly, 70*(2), 311–322.

Robertson, I. (1992). *Children, Aussie Sport and Organised Sport: Executive Summary.* South Australian Study commissioned by the Australian Sports Commission.

Smoll, F.L., & Smith, R.E. (1989). Leadership behaviors in sport: a theoretical model and research paradigm, *Journal of Applied Social Psychology, 19*(18), 1522–1551.

Usher, P. (1997). Empowerment as a powerful coaching tool, *Coaches' Report, 4*(2), 10–11.

If I had one wish for my children, it would be that each of them would reach for goals that have meaning for them as individuals.

—Lillian Carter, US nurse, first mother

A champion needs a motivation above and beyond winning.

—Pat Riley, US basketball coach

Chapter Two

Listen to the desires of your children. Encourage them and then give them the autonomy to make their own decision.

—Dennis Waitley, US motivational speaker

Rod Thorpe on Teaching Games for Understanding

This chapter contains extracts from an interview with Rod Thorpe, from Loughborough University in England. Here he gives his interpretation of empowerment as a coaching approach and discusses how Teaching Games for Understanding (TGFU, which Rod developed as Game Sense in Australia and New Zealand) fits into this coaching philosophy.

Rod Thorpe and David Bunker (1982) were central to the development of TGFU in the early 1980s. In this approach a meaningful and appropriate games experience is a key to athlete learning. It requires the coach to move from one game to another using a progressive, purposeful activity that meets the needs of athletes' learning about the actual game they play. This model breaks away from the traditional approach of isolated skill practice, where athletes learn skills of the game separate from the actual game itself (Thorpe, 1990). By playing purposeful games, athletes enjoy training and their intrinsic motivation is increased which in turn enhances their desire to learn and encourages them to continue participating in sport.

It is interesting to note that many physical education teachers and coaches were taught to save the 'game' until the end of the session, at which stage individuals could apply the techniques that they had supposedly learned. Yet as physical education teachers and coaches, many of us used to complain that the students could never get the idea of the skill when they were actually playing a game. We were trained to use games not so much for learning but as a vehicle for teaching technique, while we tended to save the game for a 'treat' at the end of the lesson. TGFU offers a more exciting approach to motivate students and to enable them to learn and enjoy themselves.

As a key developer and practitioner of TGFU, Rod discusses the movement away from the traditional approach towards a TGFU approach that enables students/athletes to learn about the game and practise the technique within the context of a game rather than separate from it. Learning in context provides a better understanding of the game as well as many opportunities for decision making, a skill that is consistently considered desirable for athletes. He also discusses how athletes learn and why TGFU enhances learning opportunities. At the end of the chapter, Rod elaborates on how skill is developed through TGFU.

The Development of Teaching Games for Understanding

Rod was first asked why he originally had the idea of Teaching Games for Understanding, when it breaks away from a traditional skill learning model:

> That is quite an interesting question, there were many interlinked reasons that came out of our thoughts on skill learning—most pertinently, the then forgotten aspects of perception and decision making, motivation, social psychology, teaching methodologies, etc. I would also add that we were taught the value of small side games as students in the early '60s, even though we were taught to focus on the 'skill' part of the lesson.
>
> When we watched youngsters playing on their own, either in a recreation setting or, say, before a practice session or lesson, we often noted quite sophisticated movements and interactions. A few examples might help:
>
> · Youngsters put some coats down to make soccer goals for a game. There are seven of them but they decide to play three, including the oldest player, against four, including the two youngest.
>
> · There is a pick-up game (play rather than organised game) of three-v-three cricket in a rural area, mixed ages. The youngsters decide to make a rule that 'The big kids can't bowl fast'.
>
> · At the start of a basketball lesson, the coach has not arrived. The youngsters are playing two-v-two and using disguise, reverse dunks (or nearly). The coach walks [in] and coaches 'fundamentals', divorced from any game or individual need. The kids were challenging themselves and each other, the coach failed to do so.
>
> The common factor in our observations was that when children were getting on with it, uncluttered by teachers and coaches, they were often more productive in terms of learning in context, enhancing motivation through challenges, social interactions, etc. They were empowered by circumstance. When it comes to empowerment I would say we noticed that kids left alone often had it and were the better for it. If we accept that well-intentioned coaching is not always better than no coaching, we might examine our practice more carefully.

What is Rod's understanding of the empowerment approach as it is used to help athletes learn?

Empowering literally means 'giving power to' and I think this is a good point to start. A coach can give power to an athlete to make decisions about all aspects of the learning and performance process. Of course the obvious [step] is to give the players the power to decide on which action to use to produce the most appropriate tactical outcome in an activity. Certainly a major push for this empowering approach at an élite level has come in activities where players have to take responsibility for decisions. I would contrast say rugby football, in which the coach is removed from the game, with American football, in which coaches dominate decision making for most players. As players become more equally fit and technically efficient there is a split-second difference in decision making. This is often linked to a split-second assessment of the relative probability of success of a number of options, a vital part to the game, for example, 'Shall I pass left and short, go myself or send the long pass right?'

But this is only a small part of empowering. The athlete can also be given power to aid motivation, self-confidence, etc. For example, 'To determine goals, what should I be aiming at in my training? How much do I think I can do? How much can I improve?' Personal goal-setting can be applied to physical and mental training, to match performances and to things like social support of teammates.

The player can also be given much more power to determine the way he/she learns. For example, when learning a shot, a tennis player might determine which sense to use to monitor a shot. Some might use the feel of the shot, some the sound of the ball on the racket, and yet others the resultant flight of the ball.

Simply, what are sometimes called the 'traditional approaches' to coaching, in which the coach is the holder of power, the font of knowledge, the provider of information, the analyser or the source of feedback, are actually disempowering. Approaches that involve the performer as an active contributor, rather than a passive receiver, most notably questioning approaches, are empowering.

Why do coaches tended to use the traditional approach that tends to disempower?

I would think a number of things contribute:

· Coaches know, and/or are supposed to know, a lot about their area and feel it is important to pass this over to the player.

· Of course ego comes into this. I cannot deny that I get a buzz out of directly helping people, it takes time to develop an approach where you get athletes to learn. Of course, it's easy to do when teaching beginners so we begin our coaching careers telling people what to do and we fail to practise early in our coaching development other methods of coaching.

· Players, parents, other coaches expect the coach to be 'delivering'.

· Most worryingly for people like me, having trained lots of teachers and coaches, when we traditionally judged coaches we would concentrate on their performance; voice projection, presence, demonstrations, appearance, preparation, etc. We did not really look at the athlete—we often gave the coach a topic. We did not assess the 'learning environment' as a whole. We also assessed a lesson or session in isolation [see next point].

· Perhaps outweighing all the other points is that the prescriptive approach produced quick 'performance' changes, within the lesson. Remember that people judged the success of their coaching on the session: 'I think that session went well'. The coaches seemed to grasp that.

· The same people would be found the following session or, after the next game, to be complaining that the players had forgotten everything: 'Don't you remember what we did?' Of course they didn't [remember] because we taught for rapid performance change, not for deep-rooted learning.

Rod was asked how this empowerment philosophy relates to the use of TGFU:

There was no more obvious an example of disempowerment than in traditional games lessons in schools, or similar coaching lessons. Children were provided with a lesson of warm-up – skill – game dominated by 'technical instruction'. The teacher chose the skill (better called 'technique' as it rarely had any perceptual, decision-making or contextual elements) and presented it often with little reference to the game it was to be used in. Clear demonstrations were applauded, despite the fact that in many cases, a good percentage of the children could not really aspire to the 'perfect model' being presented and practice ensued. Conformity was expected. If practice of the technique was 'good' in the sense of behaviour, rather than performance or improvement, the children were rewarded with a game. What little teaching occurred in the game was normally in the form of directions from the teacher as to where to stand and what angle to run at, or more often what not to do.

Lessons of this type were punctuated with 'When can we have a game?' during the technique teaching, and looks of anguish when the only bit of freedom gained, in the game, was interrupted by the instructions from the teacher. Power lay completely with the teacher.

Teaching Games for Understanding was a reaction to this 'traditional instruction' in two ways:

· we could not understand how we could expect children to learn if they were not involved in the learning process and did not understand what they were trying to do; and moreover

·   as sport psychologists, Dave Bunker and I could not continue to accept an approach in which children lost the motivation to play and improve.

We wanted an approach that we felt youngsters could contribute to, know what they were doing and where they were going. We found most children pre-12 years of age wanted to 'play', so we wanted to capture and keep this personal (intrinsic) motivation. We wanted to challenge and we wanted improvement and we realised we could not achieve any of these things if we continued to deliver a technical model, suitable for the average, using a 'prescriptive' style.

The value of questioning and problem-solving approaches in education had been well researched by the 1960s and 'educational gymnastics', an approach using problem solving, had been proposed. Games set problems; we don't even have to use words to set the problem.

Our answer was always to let children enter the game (after a warm-up). The game was suitable for their age and development and so in the model we used the term 'game form'. (Often our children would play several simpler games before they reached the mini-game typified by Aussie Sport and Kiwi Sport in their early forms.) We wanted to avoid the need for the teacher/coach to do too much 'management' which we often saw as opening up the prescriptional approach [see Playsport below].

So we set out a different format (model). We wanted to be sure the children understood the game they were playing: 'What am I trying to do?' So the games had to be simple and we included game appreciation, before we moved to tactical awareness. As children exploited the simple games, e.g. 'Coach, he/she holds the ball and we cannot get it', [their experience] might lead the children to introduce a three-second hold rule in netball.

The key element of the approach, however, is to design games that help children arrive at tactical understanding for themselves. Well-structured games give options, so that decisions have to be made. The teaching/coaching of youngsters, as with all their learning, is to give them just the right amount of option. When we have made the decision, we have to act, but that action will be different according to physical ability (of course, ability influences the decision in the first place), hence teachers and coaches must be helping their players differentially.

When Rod introduced the TGFU approach to Australia, the name became Game Sense. What is the difference between Game Sense and Teaching Games for Understanding?

I am not sure, as some use the phrase interchangeably, [that] there is much difference, but I see Game Sense as incorporating more than the original Teaching Games for Understanding. It is important, however, to think through carefully what, as a coach, you mean by a phrase like this. Len Almond, a colleague at Loughborough, often used the phrase 'Game-Centred Games Lessons' to try to put the game back at the centre of the lesson. I saw this as useful, but it only described the structure of the lesson and it hid a philosophy. My central aim in the lesson was to ensure children 'understood' what they were doing and learned more about games. Let us look first at TGFU as this was in sense the starting point.

Teaching Games for Understanding was literally an approach in which we wanted children to understand:

· the game they were playing;

· what they were trying to do;

· why they might select a particular move/action;

· that you could play games with varying degrees of competitiveness;

· that there were no universal right and wrong answers. (The phrase of TGFU is 'it all depends': it depends on the opponent's move, it depends on your position on court, it depends on how much skill you have, it depends on the situation, etc.);

· why they might want to learn and practise skills; and subsequently

· that success was there for everyone, but depended on them not the teacher or coach who could only help.

TGFU was based on recognising underlying 'principles' of games, based on space and time. Tactical understanding was reduced to simple ideas that might cross games. A goalkeeper 'bisecting the angle' is only doing what a tennis player does when covering a shot from one wing of the court. It was a simple idea, but new to many teachers and coaches.

To expand on an innovative way of enabling teachers and coaches to learn about TGFU and use the model confidently, Rod and a research assistant designed Playsport. It may be this development that helps us understand the difference between Game Sense and TGFU:

It became obvious in the late '80s that, whilst many teachers saw the value of this model for teaching games, leaders, beginner coaches and many primary (non-specialist) teachers felt they did not know games well enough to teach in this way. Playsport was a series of mini games in a number of sports presented with instructional cards, which were designed to provide children, parents and teachers with progressive, easily used programmes. The cards had clear pictures of children playing the games, with a minimal [number] of rules, safety points and suggested progressions. They used equipment as appropriate to children.

The key element was [that] the games provided progressive challenges to understanding, decision making, skill demand, social interaction, etc. but the novice teacher, mum or dad could use them without knowing the intricacies of any of these factors—they were literally providing a play structure for the children. The 'game designers' had done the thinking as to the outcomes of this play.

The Youth Sports Trust (UK), with headquarters at Loughborough University, used these [Playsport games] as their basis for TOP play and TOP sport developing equipment bags and in-service training to match. They decided that marketing the 'starter' games in Playsport that were not really a recognised sport would be more meaningful [if they were presented] as 'TOP play', and as the games became 'recognisable', they would be called TOP sport and lead on to and beyond the mini-game.

The games can be operated with minimal knowledge of the sport as they are based on child-centred play. Children learn as they meet the challenges of the 'new' (but only slightly changed) next game. Games set problems, children solve them.

In a sense TGFU expects the teacher/coach to be able to frame the challenges and to react to the situation; Playsport (TOP play/TOP sport) does not. It should be said, however, that once teachers (dare I say particularly those teachers with no previous ideas of coaching) become comfortable in the 'play' situation, they start to ask the sort of questions that are obvious within the game.

And so to the southern hemisphere. Between 1994 and 1998 I developed a programme called Game Sense with teachers and coaches in Australia and the Australian Coaching Council produced a video and instructional booklet. I should acknowledge that there were many teachers and coaches using similar approaches already, some as a result of TGFU. Whilst Game Sense is an Australian programme, it embraces elements of both TGFU and TOP sport.

Simply it *makes sense to play games'* (TOP sport), because we learn as we play. (In my opinion the teacher/coach who presents children with a well-designed game, appropriate to age and ability, is doing far more good than one who struggles to try and teach a technique or rigid tactic.) This can be followed by the *'making sense of games'* phase, that is based on teaching games for understanding.

Once primary teachers and coaches have gained confidence from the well-designed cards and children are active in TOP sport, the skills of the teacher soon appear. Children are asked 'where they are aiming and why'. The first steps to Teaching Games for Understanding are not difficult if teachers and coaches understand they are not expected to know everything or to give detailed technical instruction. Indeed, I find primary teachers are very comfortable with this teaching style.

Interestingly, whilst the Australian video is called Game Sense, much of the video is about empowerment, it leans heavily on questioning and player owner-ship. Some coaches even see the approach as important because of this change of style rather than the idea of understanding.

One of the strengths of the empowerment approach, as highlighted by coaches and players, is the strong team culture it can create. Rod was asked to elaborate on how the use of TGFU contributes to team culture:

Sports psychologists will tell you that two sources of motivation keep coming out at the top of why people play sport. One is achieving—doing something well (not surprising then that children who are not physically gifted drop away from activities which emphasise only the technical and physical). The other is 'affiliation'—being with others, interacting, friends, the social aspects. Clearly, sessions in which children, or élite sports performers, interact together are the most motivating, the very essence of teaching games for understanding.

Everything from rules to tactics to goal setting to team selection (and I do not mean picking sides in public) can involve interactions between players. They share success and they share failure, they learn how to get the best out of everybody, but we do it while children are young. The players introduce rules into games, or conditioned games (when older), and understand about the need for rules and officials. (Rules are things to help you play the game better, not things a referee uses to stop you doing things.) Perhaps most importantly, particularly at high levels, because players are given freedom to ... decide on actions, their teammates are tolerant of inappropriate decisions, and learn how to remedy and counter the potential negative consequences. Nonconformity and individuality [are] accepted, as long as it fits within a grand plan, but the grand plan has to be mutually agreed.

Of course, there will be disagreements, but this is in itself a learning process. I often ask the teacher/ coach first using small-sided games and a TGFU ap-proach: 'If you see one game stop and children disagreeing what do you do?' For me, as long as you perceive no anger or distress in the situation, stand back for a few seconds and they will often solve it. Much of my philosophy is that players, particularly games players, learn much from 'play', not least how to work together. My concern is that with directive coaches and organised play, we lose some of the potential to learn about social interaction.

This learning idea spreads to leadership, captaincy, etc. Normally, someone has to make the final decision, e.g. 'Let's do this'. The tough call for the coach is to determine at what point the coach decides and at which point he/she leaves this to the players. We do have to be careful because players want to feel con-fident about what they are doing and so someone has to cement the ideas. There is some evidence that players like a more democratic coach in training, but prefer the coach to become a wee bit more autocratic toward competition time. The skill of coaching is getting this balance right. Confused players doing their own thing is not what an empowering process is all about.

Rod was asked to relate, with reference to his experience and research, how students and top-level athletes have responded to TGFU:

At school level, there is ample evidence that more of the children enjoy this form of lesson, and skill learning does not suffer. Children with low physical ability and/or disabilities can achieve because a specific physical movement is never an essential. Games are relative, i.e. we play against another person [or other people] for an outcome.

When speaking to coaches, I often use the phrase, 'You can play games well/ badly'. What I mean is that I watch people with relatively poor techniques totally engrossed in [playing] a game of badminton. They have good tactical understanding, are totally absorbed, dash about the court and leave the session satisfied and want to come back next week. So? The toughest call for a coach is to decide 'not to do anything'. I know I could make them better players, but is it the right time to step in? Will I have enough time to ensure that my input will be positive? The coach who steps in and explains what a player is doing wrong, or shows a 'better' way is having a very negative effect if they do not have the time to spend or the player does not have the ability to incorporate a lasting improvement into their 'fun' game. This said, some would argue that the traditional lessons that do this are not well taught which results in poor responses to lessons by children, rather than the approach [as such] being incorrect.

It is important to remember that TGFU is a curriculum model that assumes some transfer between games and embraces a desire that children at least 'appreciate' what is involved in games. Many children enjoy the movement between games, particularly in the early years. The community coach who lets children play with the ideas of hitting to space and running in a rounders game, has only to introduce kicking instead of hitting to give a whole new game with common tactical principles. Little kids need change.

Top-level coaches who use the TGFU approach say to me that they feel players are better motivated and make better decisions (but they *would* say this to me). Players see that they can learn from other games and that it helps players to see beyond the 'prescribed' tactics of their own game. Because perception and decision making [are] a central focus, it is almost obvious that these qualities, often neglected in early coaching, are seen to improve.

The recognition that 'techniques are only means to an end' has also given some coaches more comfort when dealing with a nonconventional 'technical' player. Sometimes, particularly early on, we do things which some would see as 'sacrilege'. [For example,] we let rugby players run sideways, giving up the tackle line, so that they can assess their personal running potential against an opponent who has also been assessed. Of course, I might argue that the critical time for a rugby team is to defend the ruck or maul behind the tackle line that would result from an inappropriate lateral run. Mmmm.

The one certainty is that players at top level need continuous challenge. Training can get boring in a long season. The great players are students of their game and self-motivated. Of course, they will enjoy this sort of coaching and their tactical decision making will be enhanced.

Many coaches explain that these ideas of empowerment and TGFU are fantastic, but admit they do have neither confidence nor ability to put these approaches into action. Rod was asked what advice he would give to coaches who have never tried TGFU, so that they gain the confidence to begin to use such an approach:

Remember there is no 'right way' to coach, just as there is no single 'right way' to play. You will choose coaching methods to suit your persona. This said, just as a good player does not try only one method of beating an opponent, so a coach should develop a range of approaches. Consider adding this to your coaching portfolio and then decide if it works better for you. I am convinced that the traditional way has shortfalls, but I am quite willing to accept that many coaches will employ it at some points as part of a variety of approaches. Once you do this and see the 'power' of empowering, you may start to develop a philosophy which is much more about developing the player as a whole, and I do mean as a person as well as a sports performer.

Start small. You will have a well-tried coaching model in your head from your previous experience as a coach and very powerfully from the way you were coached. See if you cannot introduce elements into your sessions in which you give more freedom to players. We are all familiar with conditioned games. Choose one, but instead of diving in and telling the players how to exploit this, let them see what they can do. In a conditioned team game take out two key players from one side. Let both sides work out how to cope. It's only a five-v-three game, but let them work it out. Set a timed two-minute game, let them work out a scoring system that is fair; e.g. the three[-person] side gets five points for a goal or try, the five[-person] side gets one point. In a game of badminton or tennis, put 'no go' (for tennis ball or shuttle) zones on the court, let's see how they cope.

We have all done it, but what we usually do is select the activity that allows us, the coach, to 'tell' the players what we want them to do. The major difference is that we help them work out what they have to do to exploit the situation and this means 'questioning' either verbally or by setting a new condition in the game.

Play small-sided games, but see if you cannot select those [games] that allow you to observe decision making. Get used to trying to see what the player is basing the decision making on, watch the opponents first and then see if the response is correct, rather than only watching your player. We do it in when analysing matches; do we do it enough in practice?

For any coaching approach, we must address the possible challenges or pitfalls. On TGFU Rod suggested the following issues:

Uncertainty. Coaching is a performance and, just as players can be confused by too much information or uncertainty, so can coaches. I have always said that I am perfectly happy if presenting an alternative has made coaches think, has produced reflective coaches. I have always been concerned that many coaches tend to settle into a comfort zone about the way they coached, even if they were diligent about the latest technical, tactical, conditioning or psychological developments.

It follows, however, that whilst experienced coaches have the confidence to try things, we must not [over]load the beginner coach, hence the reason for the TOP sport concept. Equally, whilst I believe that children might learn far more in a game than in some 'technical' lessons I have seen, I do not want teachers and coaches to see this as an excuse for 'giving them a game'.

Considerable time has to go into the games and practices designed to produce a particular outcome. At times the coach can seem to be somewhat redundant, as he/she watches and assesses, only to go away and spend hours thinking how best to get 'learning outcomes' from his or her players. We all know that in games coaching, … the coach who can assess what is needed … is the most effective coach. This type of approach needs the coach to both do this and then to think how to achieve this whilst not taking responsibility away from the players.

Someone said you have to be a good coach to coach this way. Of course you do and this is what we should be aspiring to. Coaching is a 'profession'—note the small 'p' (i.e. not always for money). We need to study our profession. And if this approach and the whole issue of empowerment has not convinced you of the need to look toward this type of coaching, the fact that the commercial world is now looking at this sort of approach to increase 'performance' in their workforce must say something.

How Skill Develops Using TGFU

Many coaches suggest that if athletes work too much in games, there is no opportunity for them to learn skill. It is difficult to convince coaches that skill learning is part of the process of becoming self-aware and a game-like experience provides the stimulus to learn the skill. So Rod was asked for his opinion on this attitude, with reference to skill acquisition theory:

Of course, because people see the emphasis shifting to perception (reading the game) and decision making, based on players having knowledge and gaining responsibility for training and performance, people inevitably say to me, 'So you are not as interested in skill'. *Wrong*. If you don't have the skills to exploit the situations you are faced with, your performance has to be limited.

Rod was asked if he believed that people must have the skills before they can play the game. He responded:

No. I think we have to develop games that ensure that skills occur and develop in context. I have, over time, entered debate with the 'fundamental skills lobby', people who believe we should give our children a good grounding in fundamental skills. As a physical education student in the early '60s, I was presented with 13 fundamental skills and I firmly believe we should encourage youngsters to master these. I do, however, believe that we master these skills by having lots of goes, so we have to provide our youngsters with lots of interesting ways to practise these [skills]. And games do this.

My approach to throwing for accuracy would be to let youngsters try to, for example, throw a ball into a bucket and at a circle on the wall (targets in the horizontal and the vertical planes—maybe some readers can see how these two targets prepare youngsters for later). I would watch the efficiency of the action and help the youngsters having 'particularly obvious' problems. The children are playing a game; I am observing and helping the skill.

It is why I am so convinced that the secret to good games skills is the development of progressive games for youngsters. Games use the skills as mastered to date, but allow refinement of that skill ready for the next game. I think those of us who developed a 'games first' approach always felt that if players understood what they were trying to do and 'wanted to learn' the skill to do it, we would have far more motivated people addressing the skill problem.

Once people are well motivated, do coaches then break out into the typical technical phase of the lesson, albeit perhaps following the game? For example, your session might be structured as: warm-up, game, skill interjection, game, skill interjection, and game:

Interesting how you use two words almost interchangeably—the typical *technical* lesson and skill interjection. Remember I see 'technique' as the physical movement and 'skill' as the movement in context. I am happy to say I might break out into a *skill interjection*. Rarely will I spend time on an isolated *prescribed technique*, as we used to, because I do not think it is the best way to become skilful.

Let us look at one or two ideas that are presented by people who have studied skill acquisition (learning). Many of us, teachers and coaches, realised many years ago that isolated drills transferred poorly to games. Recent skill acquisition findings would suggest that this is due to three major reasons.

1. Integration

The relationship between the environment and the physical movement is far more integrated than we previously thought. The idea that we see something, make a decision and then select a specific action is naïve.

Let us try and give a very simple illustration. How is [it] that someone can pass the ball in basketball when falling? They have to pick up signals from their surroundings but their eyes are much lower than usual. They will release the ball in half a second when they are much lower, so they have to compute this; the arms will have to move a little differently and they will be passing up more so need a little more power. They must make sure the body hits the floor safely, and so on and so on. Of course perception and movement are integrated, so why are we surprised that a technique practised in isolation does not transfer to the game? The example does not do justice to the work of those scientists investigating skill acquisition, but perhaps does enough to convince the coach that we have to consider more carefully how we deal with 'technical' elements.

Of course, the speed with which we have to respond in games means that these links between perception and response have to be done in a split second—some would say automatically (autonomously). It is interesting to note the problems that exist when adults are suddenly asked to 'think' about the decisions they make. The thinking mind is far too slow, the moment has passed, it has to be more 'automatic' and so the importance of building this sort of approach from [when athletes are] very young is obvious.

2. Variable practice

The idea that as soon as a person has grasped the 'idea' of a skill, the practice should be varied has been in the literature for many years and yet we still see the tennis coaches feeding a constant feed for hours after hours, often with a ball machine. The literature would tell us that as soon as the basic idea of the shot is in place, then we should be building variable feeds, send one shorter, one longer, have targets near the net that require less hitting force, or more spin, etc. It seems so logical and the evidence is there, but why don't we do it?

Perhaps the answer lies in how we measure improvement. It gets right to the issue of why some coaches are reluctant to change. In a sense the skill-learning issues are not dissimilar to the empowering issues. Coaching is a long-term process but is often judged on short-term results. Let me give you one more example.

3. Memory

A researcher (Helen Wright), when doing her Masters degree at Loughborough, replicated a laboratory experiment in a basketball class. She had one group of boys learn a skill with the teacher giving information and feedback throughout the session. A parallel group, matched so she could compare, were given the same information and feedback for half the session time, but were left alone to practise on their own for the other half. Her results replicated most of what was found in the laboratory experiment. At the end of the lesson, the group with continuous teacher support was significantly better than the half-session teaching group but after a week this difference had disappeared and the group [who were] given some time to practise alone had retained more from the first lesson. The sports scientists would say that the parallel group had 'subjective reinforcement': they had to pay attention for themselves to feelings in the body, results of actions, etc. They had been actively involved in building up the memories, not relying on the teacher feedback.

If you are interested in memory, you will also be aware that some of the problem is in retrieving something from your memory: [e.g.] 'Oh I know that person—what is her name?' It is interesting to look at another very well-researched area hinted at above. Coaches may identify two aspects to work on following a match. Let us say [the aspects identified are] the short serve in doubles badminton and defence on the smash. Typically, the coach will work on one (short serve) as a block until he/she feels it is okay and then move onto the next (defence of the smash).

Research into massed/distributed, constant/random [i.e. skill acquisition theory] would suggest this [approach] is not appropriate for learning. The results are good in the session, but do not seem to last. One explanation is that if we spend some time on serve, then move to defence, then return to serve, back to defence, etc., every time we return to, say, the serve we have to try to pull it out of memory, the work on defence of the smash has pushed it out of our thoughts. Can you see the links to the Helen Wright example?

We can make very fast improvements in the performance of a skill in a single session, but this might be disadvantaging the long-term learning process. The parallel with direct teaching, in which some rapid short-lived improvements can be made, and questioning-type approaches, in which immediate improvement is less obvious, must be seen. And thereby lies the problem.

Community coaches say to me, 'But the players (and parents of young players) expect me to tell them their faults (negative) and to rectify them quickly in a single session.' Professional club coaches say to me, 'I agree with you but if I do not get a quick return on my efforts I will be out.'

We have to change the way we evaluate coaching—coaching is a long-term process concerned with the development of a player. I think many coaches are really instructors.

Rod was asked to link all these thoughts about skill learning with ideas on coaching games and empowerment:

I think two key messages come through this.

One is that players have to be involved in the learning process, sometimes consciously: [ask them,] 'What are you trying to do?' Sometimes [they should be involved] subconsciously, by providing game like situations that bring into play an integrated response to the situation.

The second [message] is that many of the games children develop when left to their own devices, in a play-like environment, provide better learning experiences than the situations we, as supposedly knowledgeable coaches, have evolved. In coach training we have concentrated on how we coach and neglected how our performers learn.

For skill learning, I become more and more convinced that the secret is to 'condition/modify' games to the extent that the 'movement' required occurs more often, but does so under varying conditions. This does not stop the coach clarifying when [he or she is] certain this will help: 'If you spread the fingers, you will have more control on the volleyball during the volley'. [However, this idea does suggest] that the sooner a practice can be put into more realistic game-like situations, the better.

References

Bunker, D., & Thorpe, R.D. (1982). A model for the teaching of games in secondary schools, *Bulletin of Physical Education, 18*(1), 5–8.

Thorpe, R. (1990). New directions in games teaching. In Armstrong, N. *New Directions in Physical Education*, pp. 79–100. Champaign, IL: Human Kinetics.

Note

For those interested in the theoretical aspects of this work, research is ongoing in many countries, under the heading of TGFU and/or Game Sense. TGFU is essentially practical so coaches should contact their own sporting bodies, coaching associations and local universities and colleges to see if work is being done in this area.

To implement this type of approach, coaches can access a range of resources including:

Australian Sports Commission (1997). Game Sense: Developing Thinking Players: A Presenter's Guide and Workbook. <www.ausport.gov.au>

Griffith, L.L., Mitchell, S.A., & Oslin, J.L. (1997). Teaching Sport Concepts and Skills: A Tactical Games Approach. Champaign, IL: Human Kinetics.

Information about the TOP programmes can be gained from the Youth Sports Trust, Loughborough University, Loughborough, Leicestershire LE11 3TU, England. For research information, contact the Institute of Youth Sport at the same address.

*I never learn anything talking.
I only learn things when I ask
questions.*

     —Lou Holtz, US football coach

*Children's talent to endure stems from
their ignorance of alternatives.*

     —Maya Angelou

Chapter Three   *'Coach', he whispered. His voice shook just a trifle. 'I found it, coach, the thing you wanted me to learn for myself.'*

—Schoolboy, 'Split seconds: Tales of the Cinder Track 1927', Sports Council 1991

An Empowering Coach: Case Study of Wayne Smith

The purpose of this chapter is to discuss the coaching approach developed and used by Wayne Smith, the current coach of the All Blacks (the New Zealand national men's rugby team). A prime proponent for the empowering philosophy, Wayne Smith is noted for his ability to formulate a team culture that is more successful than that produced by traditional rugby approaches in the modern era.

An empowering approach, as suggested in Chapter One, is ideal for sports teams as it gives athletes control and choice, it enables them to make decisions while competing, and it brings back the 'fun' of participating in sport because athletes have greater internal motivation. As well as using an empowerment approach with élite rugby squads, Wayne has used it when coaching children. His philosophy, vision and values can take rugby, in his case, into the 21st century.

Wayne was interviewed at length while he was still coaching the Canterbury Crusaders (a New Zealand regional men's rugby team that plays in the Super 12 international rugby competition), before he took up his position with the All Blacks. After he became All Blacks coach, Wayne edited and added to many of his quotes from the original interview; therefore some of his experience from his time with the national team is integrated here. The chapter begins by focusing on how Wayne has developed his empowerment philosophy. Wayne then discusses his own development as a coach and reasons for adopting Game Sense, the advantages and implementation of such an approach, and the process of empowering players. He also covers some of the challenges he faces in using an empowerment approach and how he will use it with the All Blacks.

Wayne's Philosophy on Coaching

Wayne's coaching philosophy, with its strong emphasis on empowerment principles, was briefly introduced in Chapter One. In this section he elaborates on the essential elements of his philosophy.

To give some background to the development of his philosophy, Wayne discusses the contribution of the players to the team. He prefers people on his team to show real *character*, which he suggests is:

> ... the ability to persist, be relentless and not give up when the chips are down ... the ability, when away from home, when faced with adversity, when conditions are against them and they haven't got their star player, to still perform with character, with persistence. People with character don't look for the easy way out or for excuses when up against it, they achieve the unexpected. They leave a little bit of themselves on the field every time they play and they take responsibility for their own performance.

Building character among a group of players, so that they take responsibility for their preparation and performance, is part of the foundation of an empowerment approach. Wayne also suggests that every member of his team (whether he is a wing or loose forward) should have the ability to be a leader who can communicate what he is seeing on the field, where to go, what space he is in and what the opposition is doing. All players should have the ability to 'see that, to understand that, to call it, to react to it'.

Wayne believes in traditional values, so he looks at the values that have been associated with great teams of the past. If the players take on those values (i.e. by living them), then a great environment is created.

Wayne's philosophy also relates to the importance of developing the whole person, not just the rugby player. He suggests that a focus on career goals is a key to developing thinking people that are able to empower themselves by encouraging them to study, work or help in the community (see Chapter Seven). Wayne believes that personal development is extremely important:

> I am a coach that likes to learn and believes that learning faster than the others is critical. I communicate that attitude to the players, making sure that they also are open to new ideas. Players generally like innovation, but it's important they treat everything on merit. You've got to be prepared to make mistakes and allow your players to make them. The team that makes the most mistakes wins the game because only 'doers' make them. Your job as coach is to ensure they're not making the same mistakes over and over.

Another key area in Wayne's coaching approach is his belief that the principle of honesty with players is extremely important. He believes that it is essential to act on this principle, not just talk about it:

Being honest with the players is crucial. We establish a protocol where we expect people to 'stab in the belly', not the back. Telling players why they are not playing on the weekend is fundamental to achieving an honest, up-front team environment. I like to back my selectorial opinion with statistical and video evidence, making suggestions on what the player should work on to get a starting spot in the team. The players will often react out of disappointment, and say 'I can do these things, give me an opportunity'. A player [at the regional level] once suggested I was using different standards to measure him than I was using to assess the other player in his position. He was right. We named him to start the following game, and he was outstanding. He is now an All Black.

To be successful, you need players with a hungry attitude to accept the challenges you set them. Then, when you do give them an opportunity, they will have worked on their weaknesses and you can say to them, 'You know what the team needs from you, you've now got an opportunity to perform'. You establish your expectations and stick to them. If [the players] don't come up to scratch, you need to help them improve until they do. Worthwhile people seldom let you down if you are up-front and honest with them.

While Wayne was coaching the Canterbury Crusaders from 1997 to 1999, the team won two Super 12 championships. His empowerment approach with the Crusaders was innovative. Many of the players had never been coached in this way. Wayne became a leader in rugby coaching by learning how to empower players. His example has provided encouragement for many coaches of rugby (and other sports), who are now beginning to learn about and use an empowerment approach.

One of the first steps in initiating such an approach is to set up a team of people to help empower the players. Wayne sees the merit of finding the right people for the job:

You should spend the time to get the right people around you. You need the right players, obviously, and the best support staff you can get. Getting the right people going in the right direction is important. You need a really strong vision that everyone is part of formulating. Ensure the best systems and processes are set up, commit to excellence and consistent work habits, develop a hard mental attitude and smother it all in good, old-fashion values. I reckon if you have all those things, you'll at least get satisfaction as an outcome.

Getting the right people for the Crusaders was fundamental to our success. I've been fortunate in having people like Peter Sloane and Steve Hansen as my coaching partners. I've also got other people around me who are able to teach and learn. We work well together. We enjoy what we are doing. Often you neglect the journey in your eagerness or anxiety about reaching a goal. John Wooden (ex-UCLA basketball coach) said, 'A successful journey becomes your destination'. Try and make your journey better than the inn.

Wayne indicates that having a great bunch of people to learn from is a major part of developing a successful team (as well as contributing to his own development as a coach—the subject of the next section):

> Gilbert Enoka is really helpful as an educator. When I was playing, we got him along to talk to the Canterbury team the night before a Ranfurly Shield match. He spoke to us about the mental side of rugby ... I become convinced ... a psychological skills training [PST] programme was important. I went on to develop my own PST programme as a player with Gilbert's guidance. Once I became coach, I reintroduced him to the team. Now, he is an integral part of the Crusaders and All Black set-ups, not just in PST, but just as importantly in time management and game review systems.

It seems obvious that Wayne has been successful in obtaining the right people to develop the Crusaders and the All Blacks. His staff are teachers and keen learners. His players have become learners of the game and of life by being empowered to take ownership of their direction and reasons for playing rugby.

As part of the empowerment process and giving players ownership of the game, Wayne also believes in the 'rotation' system of play whereby all players have an equal opportunity to be selected for particular games:

> You've got people on the team that you selected, so you've got to give them the opportunity. You have to trust that they can do it. At some stage you are going to need them. Also, the players who are starting players, so to speak, need that competitive guy behind them. They need to know that people are keeping them honest. You need to receive the message that someone is ready to step into your spot if your performance drops.

Wayne's Development as a Coach

Wayne has a passion for rugby. After finishing his playing career with the All Blacks (1980–1985), he saw it as an obvious progression to coach the game he loved. In 1986 he went to Italy to play for a club. He learned Italian and was thrown in the deep end when he began to coach an Italian team:

> When I went to Italy, I'd already been an All Black and a captain of the New Zealand Sevens team for which I took almost a player/coaching type role along with a very open coach, Bryce Rope ... (Bryce took the team up to Hong Kong and we won, the first time ever). Most of our team [had] never really played the game, as 15-aside rugby is much more important in New Zealand. I took responsibility for researching the game. I read books about Sevens ... I made sure I understood the fundamentals of the game ... The experience gave me the knowledge that I could research things. I was open to learning, wasn't threatened by the fact that I knew little about the game. I was quite prepared to do my homework to ensure I was giving it the best shot I could.

Wayne has continued to use research as a major form of developing his coaching. He believes a coach can never stop learning. He also realises that the way he played and was coached is not necessarily the best way for the modern game:

> When I went to Italy, I had a situation where I couldn't speak the language and I had players who had grown up in a different system to mine. Putting them through the sort of trainings that I had been used to wasn't going to motivate them, wasn't going to work. I wanted to get the most out of the opportunity. So I had to adjust pretty quickly to what I call a global coaching methodology, which in its pure sense is playing the game, rather than analytically developing individual techniques. The French coaching influence in Italy had developed a style of coaching based on opposed situations where the coach introduces the ball according to which game situation he wants to simulate.

Wayne clarifies the idea of a *global methodology* to coaching:

> If you look at a range of coaching methodologies, 'analytical' would be on one end of the spectrum and 'global' on the other. Using an analytical methodology you'd say, 'Put your foot there, put your hand there, drop your shoulder and finish up in this position'. Global would be saying, 'This player has the ball, stop him from scoring a try', ... just doing it, then letting them sort out the most effective way themselves. I think effective coaching moves up and down this spectrum.

Wishing to develop his coaching further, Wayne began to think about the empowering type of approach from his experiences of coaching in Italy. The factors motivating his learning were:

> ... experience and a realisation that to survive I had to change. I had to adapt to what they'd [Italians] been used to. So I fell into it really, but I went into it with an openness to adapt rather than change them from what they had been used to. I then brought in some of my analytical [tools] ... That was probably what they were looking for to make the difference within their play. They wanted to bring some of the All Blacks' ways into their framework.

A large part of Wayne's initial coaching development was observing the Italian coaches:

> I went and watched coaches who literally threw the ball in the air and two teams played, tackling each other as they would in a game. It was very unstructured but I thought that I could adapt and improve this style. I developed activities that had one area of a field strongly defended, then threw the ball to the attacking team to see if they could figure out the space and make some ground. That's a situation in the game that's real. I modified the approach to develop my own style. I was still telling them what to do and where to go, but at least I had started developing this raw game sense type approach.

This approach reflects elements of the Game Sense approach discussed by Rod Thorpe in Chapter Two. Rod developed the use of game-like situations in which players learn about technique and tactics of the actual game. Game Sense allows the development of greater intrinsic motivation among players and more movement appropriate to the actual game for which players are being trained.

In his coaching development Wayne observed and spoke with a French coach, André Buonomo in Benetton (about 15 minutes from where he was based in Italy). Admiring and seeing some real worth in André's empowerment approach to coaching, Wayne decided, 'This is for me, this is the way to mix the analytical side with game simulation side'. As he continued to learn from André's model, he began to use a similar approach in his own coaching. Questioning was a big part of André's approach and Wayne too began learning how to question. Wayne returned to coach in Italy from 1992 to 1994. It was at this time that he started using and continuing to learn about empowerment at a more élite level.

After returning from Italy, Wayne was the chief executive of Hawkes Bay Rugby from 1994 to 1997. This job enabled him to think further about and develop empowerment in a different context. When taking up this job, he accepted a new challenge and a new area of learning was involved:

> It was at a time they were reconstituting the union and they wanted to set up a board structure. I had no skills in that area at all, so it was a huge learning curve for me. I had to learn about change management, how to set up systems and how to facilitate meetings.
>
> I picked up skills mainly through the board members who are exceptional business people. They educated me. They taught me to apply myself to become a little better every day. They helped me develop a systematic approach to running a project, a team or a business. The job taught me about the processes a team [organisation] needs to put in place, like how to set goals and review them. The role really fitted in closely with what we do as coaches, so it was a great learning experience for me. I read a lot of corporate-type coaching and business management books. Complementing our traditional values, rugby's heritage, with a vision-driven process and systems-based model is the way ahead. Learn from the past, but don't live in the past.

Wayne talked further about the many books he read, which combined with his professional experience in helping him to think about and set up his empowering approach:

> I read books like The Tao of Coaching [Landsberg, 1996] and The Flight of the Buffalo [Belasco & Stayer, 1993], about empowering people, giving them ownership of their responsibilities to perform. This is an ongoing education process

really and by the time I was ready to apply for the Crusaders job, I felt I was ready to combine the coaching methodology I had developed with the skills I learned running a business.

Wayne was asked what his advice would be for coaches who are interested in learning about an empowering approach:

The key thing I think is the openness to learning. I think coaches need to look at things on merit and understand that just because they've played the game, they don't know everything about it. This is particularly so in sports like rugby where laws are changing all the time. Having a passion to improve is important. Knowing that you are part of the problem means you can also be part of the solution.

As part of the journey to discover solutions and search for best practices, Wayne created the 'crow's nest', an innovative way to look into the future:

Every season we put groups in the 'crow's nest' and they look into the future to see how the laws are going to affect the game … They report back on how they think teams will play, what new styles will develop. Knowing this means you can adapt to meet changes before they happen. It's important to innovate, to be flexible and understand that you don't know everything, that there is more than one way to skin a cat.

An issue that Wayne reiterated extensively in the interview was that he is still learning about coaching and about how to use an empowerment approach. Coaches always need to be developing, learning and asking plenty of questions. On his own learning, Wayne says:

I am always trying to do things better. Progress for me is not going back to my natural or learned instincts from years of being coached in a certain way. The tendency for me under pressure is to bark out orders and say, 'Do it this way'. Sometimes, I'll come home and think, 'I know that wasn't the way to handle that' or 'I had a poor night tonight'. That is a good thing because the next day I make a conscious effort to go back to empowering the players more. A questioning approach encourages the self-awareness that players need to get better at what they're doing. This doesn't mean you abdicate your responsibilities as a leader. You set your standards and expectations. Your job as coach is to then ensure the players come up to them.

Much of his thinking and development came from people who coached Wayne when he was a player:

My coach for Canterbury, Alex Wylie, had technical nous, hardness and knowledge of ' bush' psychology (he seemed to know inherently what to do). His coaching offsider, Doug Bruce, was calm, thoughtful and knew the game inside out.

My last All Blacks coach, Brian Lochore, had all these qualities. [He] had extraordinary mana as a person and the wisdom to 'know' his players. He had (still has) real credibility as one of the great All Black captains. He technically knows what he is on about, is calm, composed and steeped in the values that make the All Blacks great. You could talk anything with Brian in a social situation (not just rugby). You'd talk politics, farming or whatever. He is well rounded. He is the only All Blacks coach to win a World Cup, but it never changed him as a coach or man ... His record speaks for itself and, more importantly, he has influenced his players as people.

In his modern coaching, Wayne uses others' knowledge, including the styles and methods of other coaches, to help develop his coaching and continue his learning. He seeks the advice and information he needs, often by email. He sets up relationships with coaches and experts who can help him, such as those who use an empowerment approach, and asks many questions:

When I first committed to using empowerment in my coaching, there was no one else really using it, so I needed to look at other sports to keep learning. I still like to see what other coaches do and whether I am on the right track or not. I know the way I want to go ... to continue empowering my players and to get better at questioning.

I have to work on my ability to discriminate between the need to ask questions about the skill and the need to ask about the tactics, e.g. understand whether it's a skill issue that let the player down or whether he didn't understand the game. Did he fail to pass because he couldn't technically execute it quickly enough, or did he pass because he couldn't see what was [going] on? You can get the answer quickly ... by asking, 'What did you do?', 'What did you see?' and 'What did you want to do?' You can soon find out whether he wanted to pass and couldn't or whether he ran with it because he didn't see that the pass was on.

The skill is in understanding how to use the questions and doing it quickly and selectively so that you're observing more than talking. Let the players have a go, then if you see the activity being done correctly you don't need to step in. My biggest fault is overquestioning.

As evident from Wayne's statement, asking meaningful questions and 'reading the play' is important. (For further information on how to ask meaningful questions, see Chapter Eight.)

A key component of a coach's development and enhanced performance is *self-analysis* (see Chapter Ten). It is used by many coaches to gather feedback and reflect on what is working and what can be improved in their coaching. Wayne also believes strongly in obtaining feedback on his coaching to help him self-analyse:

I've participated in several coach evaluations. I've always tended to evaluate myself through videoing practice sessions, or by getting the players to do it.

Gilbert Enoka and Peter Thorburn are my coaching mentors. They make comments after training which help me assess how the session went in general and, more specifically, how individual activities went. They can often see things more objectively than I can.

Steve [Hansen] and I evaluated each other's coaching performance constantly. He'd often say, 'I think that activity worked, but …'. We sought each other's views and listened to them.

As part of a coach's development, it is important to get feedback from the players about the approach:

The players will give you feedback if you have the right culture. We have a simple rating system at training. I am convinced that players love learning about the game and genuinely want to improve something at every session.

Why does Wayne Use Game Sense?

Game Sense (see Chapter Two) is an approach that has become popular in New Zealand and Australia. Game Sense can be a useful tool in an empowerment approach because it encourages athletes to understand and appreciate the game. In addition, it enables them to make informed decisions, take ownership for their learning and exercise choice and control over how they play the game.

On Game Sense as a part of empowerment, Wayne says:

We never trained like that in New Zealand [using Game Sense]. The closest we came to it was pick-up games as kids. All my life we'd always trained without opposition, not really simulating game situations or pressures. [There was] no thought of where the tackle line was or what you were looking for to make the pass or run through the gap. Game Sense is a logical way to create tactical understanding and awareness, getting players making the right decisions in various situations.

The use of Game Sense enabled Wayne to begin to develop a non-traditional approach to help athletes learn. Game Sense had a great influence on his thinking and the development of his empowerment approach. Wayne admits that, before he started using Game Sense, he was a prescriptive (autocratic) coach:

I was still very much an instructional person who told them what to do, told them where to put their foot and where to put their hand when catching and how to read a situation … I was telling them how to do it. It wasn't really until I came back and got involved with kids at Kiwisport level in my job that I started to understand about learning. You can tell people how to do something until you are blue in the face, but unless they understand it or believe it themselves, they aren't going to take it on board. So, I started to ask some questions.

Then while doing some personal development …I came across David Hadfield who had written a paper called Query Theory on a questioning approach and how it created self-awareness. It was exactly the sort of support and evidence that I was looking for to say that this is the right approach. So I went from doing it ad hoc [to trying] to live by it at training.

I try to use [Query Theory] all the time, a mixture of positive reinforcement, Game Sense and a questioning approach. I don't always succeed. I'm not good enough yet to not fall back into old habits. I am also a bit reactive at times, especially when things aren't going well. Patience and composure are two virtues I am still trying to master.

The 'game' in Game Sense is a key to designing training sessions. Instead of using the traditional practice drills, which have no real relevance to the actual game, Wayne tries to design games that match the purpose of a particular drill:

I have used the Game Sense-type approach for training since 1986 when I started playing and coaching in Italy and saw the French influence. I didn't know then it was called Game Sense, but we were putting players in match-like situations then changing the rules or the situation to develop adaptation. Game Sense ensures players practise having to make decisions all the time.

If there is no purpose, a coach tends to use questioning for the sake of using questioning, which is a common occurrence when coaches are learning about Game Sense. In Game Sense, the questions should come from and be geared towards achieving an objective the coach and team have identified:

Not knowing what to achieve or not having an objective is a common fault. Questioning, for the sake of it, was a big problem I saw when reviewing a video of one of my sessions. The players participated in very little activity because I kept asking questions. Observation is a big part of a game sense approach. Look before you question so that you can be more incisive and meaningful with your queries.

When Wayne designs his training sessions, he is still learning and developing Game Sense ideas. To coaches, he suggests:

Take a drill, then try to think about how you can change the rules, the size of the field, the time limit, the scoring systems, etc., to get what you want to get out of it. I try to give [the players] a framework so that they can design their own drills. I don't have a book of drills because every time I go out there, I do something new. Drills develop from the last training and reflect what we are trying to achieve next week.

Wayne knows that his style is different and that his knowledge of rugby is quite extensive, so when planning for using games at training he says:

You don't have to do what other people do. You think of a way, e.g. if you want to work on your forwards picking the ball up and going through the middle of the defence, you create ways to spread the defence at training. They are not even drills; they're mini-games.

Advantages of Game Sense

Wayne was asked what is the biggest advantage to Game Sense within an empowerment approach to coaching. His answer also gives a practical example of how he uses questioning as a major coaching technique to ensure athletes are learning from the various games:

The biggest advantage to a Game Sense approach (opposed activities/games) is that it develops tactical awareness. You put [the players] in real game situations with similar pressures and you require them to choose the right options. It also ensures that they have the skills to make the right tactical decision.

For example, when you create three attackers against two defenders, the obvious thing would be for the second attacker to draw the last defender and pass to the outside guy because he is the one in space. If you can see that the player understands that, but cannot execute the skill, you need to ask some questions. For example:

Wayne: 'What did you do?'

Player: 'I held on to it.'

Wayne: 'Where was the space?'

Player: 'It was outside.'

Wayne: 'Why didn't you pass?'

Player: 'I couldn't get the pass away.'

Then you know it is a technical issue. You could then ask:

Wayne: 'Why couldn't you get the pass away?'

Player: 'He was on me too quick.'

Wayne: 'How could you give yourself a bit of time?'

Player: 'I would slow down.'

Wayne: 'How do you slow down?'

Player: 'Take short steps.' Or maybe it's a hand speed issue and: 'I had enough time, but I couldn't get the ball ready, it was going to be a bad pass.'

Wayne: 'Well, why didn't you have time to get your pass away?'

Player: 'I took the ball into my chest.'

Wayne: 'Where were your hands when you caught it?'

Player: 'They were out in front.'

Wayne: 'Where should they be?'

Player: 'Towards the passer. If I met the ball earlier, I could have passed it.'

So you can get them through to the answer and they come up with it … They will learn from it better than having been told the solution.

I like the approach. It is logical. Players are working on understanding the game, not just the skills required. You can work on all the skills you like, but if you can't use them in the game, you are not going to get much satisfaction.

It is also worth remembering that there are times when athletes do need to be told what to do—the trick is to identify that moment. This is part of the art of coaching, as Wayne suggests:

There are times when you need to say, 'You had more power in the tackle that time, what did you differently with your foot?'

They might say, 'I am not sure.'

Wayne: 'What did you do that time with your leading foot?'

Player: 'I put it closer to him.'

Wayne: 'So what did that do?'

Player: 'It generated more power from my front leg …'

Wayne suggests that players learn from the approach because:

… they understand it … I could tell them 10 times, 'You've got to meet the ball early', but if they have self-awareness that meeting the ball early means that you can get the pass away quicker, then they are probably going to try it a lot more quickly. The thing about questioning is that coaches need to have knowledge and good eyes. You have to be able to see the three-vs-two or the two-against-one situations.

… quite often I use a technique where I carry a second ball and I'll look and see that there are two attackers against only one defender. I will blow the whistle and throw the ball to the two attackers and see how they react and how it develops, how they play it. It is not just the skill of questioning, but it is the understanding of the game, to see it develop or be able to create it. There are a lot of skills associated with it, it's not coaching by abdication. You also need to ensure your players understand why you are using a questioning approach.

One of the benefits indicated in research about Game Sense is the ability to increase intrinsic motivation of players. Wayne agrees:

I think that definitely people are more motivated if you've got activities that are meaningful and fun … I think most of my players would say that our trainings are meaningful and interesting because I put them into game situations all the time. If it is fun and they can see the purpose behind it, it is motivating to them. They will enjoy doing it and they will do it well.

If you make [the questioning] logical and you start steering them towards learning and playing the game better then they are going to get motivated by that. If it is illogical or poorly done, it can be frustrating. Just asking questions for the sake of it is meaningless. I have days where I've had a player say to me, 'Let's just get on with it'. That means I am asking too many questions. Those are all skills that you learn as you go along.

Learning Game Sense as part of an empowerment approach is like learning any other skill. Coaches need to be prepared to trial it and search for ways to continue to develop it:

You have to understand that if you are going to use the approach, you're not going to be perfect at it: you have to keep practising it, keep learning it. It helps you expand your armoury, drills or ways of doing things. It helps you improve your own understanding of the game, as well as your players'!

Implementing an Empowerment Approach

Before his recent coaching successes, Wayne lectured about empowerment in a practicum course at Massey University. He said that at that stage, 'there was a lot of scepticism because I hadn't been coaching in New Zealand' and he lacked credibility. Nevertheless, he suggested to the students that he would use the empowering approach with the Crusaders: 'I am going to empower my players. I am going to endeavour to use a questioning type approach and a Game Sense sort of approach.'

Yet he also admits, 'there would be times where I fall back into the way I was taught.' As part of the process of learning about this approach, coaches will tend to revert to the coaching style that they received as players. Wayne reflects on why people, including himself, tend to fall back to old habits:

Sometimes it is because of frustration or time pressures, or things not going right ... we film our trainings to look at the drills we are doing and make sure they are valid, see whether the players are doing them really well and to check our way of communicating. Quite often I go home and think, 'Gee that wasn't the right way to handle that player tonight'. I've had to learn strategies to cope with people making mistakes. I have very competitive instincts and like to see everything done well. It has been an ongoing learning experience allowing the players to make errors along the way.

One of the concerns Wayne raised, from his perspective in a very public position, is that people tend to criticise something new until it has been proven (usually by winning). An empowerment approach draws away from a traditional approach (which has been considered successful), where coaches claim control and ownership of their athletes. Wayne suggests that initially the public was not convinced of his approach:

> One of the problems that I faced early on in my career was that people thought that I was too soft. We won the national Sevens when I coached the Canterbury side. It was the first time we'd ever won the nationals. I coached the team, and utilised Gilbert Enoka as sports psychologist. There was a public perception that I wasn't tough enough ... If you ask the players [now], they'd say that in my own way I am a hard coach. I preach attention to detail, expect my players to work hard and am not afraid to front [up to] them over form and selection issues. I don't want my players to be better than their opponents—I want them to be the very best they can be.

As Wayne proceeds in using empowerment, learns more and continues to improve, he gains more credibility. His approach has now become something of a goal for many coaches, but other coaches still have not been convinced. To Wayne the success of the empowering approach does not just lie in the results. He also points to the team culture it produces:

> ... we have people coming down to play from the draft who invariably put pressure on us to keep them here. They want to stay and play their rugby in Canterbury. There are other players around the country who speak highly of our organisation and they'd like to become Crusaders. I think these are the real indicators of the sort of environment that we've got.

When asked about how to lessen the emphasis on winning a game, coming first or becoming a world champion, Wayne suggests that perhaps the media and sporting bodies need to:

> ... be aware that enjoyment is going to be a critical factor in professional rugby because if players are playing only because they are getting paid, then we are already losing. Well-balanced athletes are more motivated at training. They perform better on the field and cope better with losing.
>
> Ultimately, I suggest that the best balanced teams are the ones that win anyway ... you can't guarantee winning, but what you can guarantee, if you create the right environment, is that on the paddock they will roll their sleeves up and do the best they can. If you prepare well, play with passion and enjoy what you are doing, then you'll do justice to the jersey you are playing in.

When convincing various bodies within the rugby union about empowerment, Wayne ran into some obstacles. The traditional thinking had to be challenged and Wayne offered a different approach. The Canterbury Rugby Union was happy for Wayne to 'do his thing'. Wayne has found that, 'It's only since we forged the boundaries that we have been successful'.

As coaches develop an empowerment approach, one of their most important goals will be to organise a good team environment and culture. With both the Crusaders and the All Blacks, the team culture was a major focus for Wayne. The success that came from giving it priority has been proven in many ways. One of the many techniques used to establish a team vision and attitude was a videotape based on *Henry V* (a film set during the period of the original Crusades), which Wayne, co-coach Peter Sloane and Gilbert Enoka created. This video contributed significantly to the success of the team, but at the beginning there was uncertainty:

> ... The first time we showed the team a video we had put together, was groundbreaking. The idea of the video was to set the scene prior to us facilitating our team vision, values and attitudes. To see the response at the end gave me so much confidence. It's something we'd never done before that turned out to be really powerful. The players got into the whole thing. They ended up buying into something bigger than themselves.

Wayne spoke about other ideas implemented after this first video, that were similarly designed to develop a successful team culture among the Crusaders and to empower players:

> Since then we've tried all sorts of different initiatives, we've pushed the boundaries—e.g. we've used a team song, trained in different ways, used different methodologies and encouraged our players to look to the future and adapt before the changes occur. We've also done team-building type activities in association with our vision and values.
>
> In 1999 we did something that at the time, again, I was nervous about. We undertook a wilderness experience at Mt Kosciosko in Australia. We had to climb the mountain, which could only be done with the help of your mates. We reached our peak, but we did it by working together. We contrasted this with how we had achieved success in 1998 when we had stuttered along as individuals, not really gelling as a team until it was almost too late.
>
> Whilst standing on top of the mountain I said to the players, 'You are standing on the highest point in Australia', which was significant—we had conquered Australia. Caleb Ralph was standing next to me and said, 'No, that peak over there is higher!' (There was another one about 100 metres away which was slightly higher.) Still, with a bit of imagination and symbolism, the point was made!
>
> The Kosciosko experience illustrated that to win Super 12 again, we had to pay a higher price—we'd have to all go in the same direction and help each other more. We fed these ideas throughout the season, creating a really powerful and selfless team ethic.

The Process of Empowering Players

So Wayne put all these systems in place, using an innovative type of

thinking, but what really happened? How did the players react to this approach?

I think the reaction initially by some of the players was a bit of scepticism, things like, 'This guy doesn't really know what he is going on about'. I know I had a bit of credibility problem with a couple of them initially because they wanted me to come and say, 'This is what we are going to do and this is how we are going to do it'.

They responded this way because they are used to people coming and telling them what to do and they can tell from what a coach tells them whether he knows the game or not. It took a while to establish the fact that I did know the game, that I wasn't asking questions because I didn't know the answers. I was asking for a reason.

It also took them out of their comfort zone a lot because I was trying to get tight forwards, for example, doing something that they traditionally didn't do. Rather than just carry the ball into contact and set it up, I wanted them to be able to draw and pass to get the ball into space. I did that by asking questions like, 'Where is the defence?', 'Where was the space?', 'How could you have got the ball there?'. Initially, the players really struggled with it. Props didn't see it as their job to get the ball into space. Their role in the team was to set up rucks and mauls. It took a while for them to start understanding the concept of team attack. By them knowing what we were trying to achieve and playing like the backs in certain situations, we were going to be more effective. The vice versa is true as well, i.e. backs have to know how to perform the forwards tasks at the breakdown.

There were some personalities on the team that felt that while I was questioning, I was criticising or I was bringing up negatives in their play. However, quite often, the question I asked should have had a positive response from the player because it was about a good thing that they'd done. For example:

Wayne: 'What did you do there?'

Player: 'I did the right thing.'

Wayne: 'Yes exactly, but tell me what you did.'

Player: 'I passed the ball.'

Wayne: 'Why?'

Player: 'Because that defender came in on me, so I passed to the guy that was clear on the outside of me.'

Wayne: 'Great.'

That showed me that the player understood the situation.

There are still two or three players that tend to react negatively to questioning. I think, in general, all players initially had some problems with [being questioned]. I think the activities I used were also new and different for them. They were used to doing the traditional ruck and run type practices for rugby rather than being put in game-like activities. I'd throw a ball to the attack and if they couldn't get through, I threw the ball to the defence. They had to switch roles quickly. It took a great deal of trust on the players' behalf to forgo what they had been used to (and felt comfortable with) and commit wholeheartedly to my methods. Now those same players, when they go back into a more traditional coaching environment, quite often become frustrated with the lack of learning.

Wayne also encourages input from the players:

The players will quite often come up with extensions to activities, progressions if you like. They will quite often come and say, 'Why don't we do this?', 'Why don't we put this player here and create this?' or 'Why don't we make the field bigger?' or whatever.

The players' input encourages creative thinking. The players have to play the game, so their ideas and ways of reading the game are highly relevant to training for it.

When Wayne began coaching the Crusaders, he spoke about how the players were empowered. Here he provides an account of the procedures he followed to enable players to take ownership of their learning and playing:

Pre-season, the players and coaches agree on what qualities they most need to be the best player they can (in each of physical, tactical, psychological and attitudinal areas). Then for the first month I sit down with players weekly and go through their game on video. We discuss some of the issues, we look at the statistics, then we agree where they're at and what they have to do to improve. We do check points every month to ensure they are getting ongoing improvements. Their own week-by-week reviews (using videos of the games) tend to be both skill- and situational-specific and throw up areas that they need to work on at both individual and team training sessions.

... it is a good system, but it shouldn't just be coach-directed. I want to get to a system this year where we email video clips to the players and they review the game on their own. Then they can come back and talk to me if they need to or if I need them to. We are trying to make them responsible for self-analysis, but early on I find I need to lead it, so they can learn the system.

To empower players, it is important that they gain the skills of self-awareness (see Chapter One). Athletes need to understand how and why they are performing, including in their tactics and skill development. Wayne had initial difficulties in trying to get players to become self-aware:

In the first year, they were so lacking in self-awareness that I would ask 'What did you do?' and players would have trouble remembering what they did. They played like robots. They did what they were told to do and didn't really feel their performance.

Empowering through questioning has other advantages along with increasing self-awareness among players. Questioning also focuses athletes in their thinking and thus their concentration remains consistently higher in trainings, which transfers well to the game. Wayne agrees that questioning 'really makes them aware the whole time. But also you know that your trainings can't be quite so long. It's ... hard to concentrate for long periods of time.'

Wayne suggests that sometimes players can take an empowerment approach for granted and not genuinely be empowered. One of the real arts to any coaching is to be able to read the players all the time:

> You need to recognise when the players are just going through the motions. Recognising that is an art. That is where an inexperienced person using a Query Theory and empowerment type approach might fall in a hole.

Wayne was a development officer with the Canterbury Rugby Union from 1989 to 1992. In this job, he was responsible for teaching various courses to coaches and teachers. He taught children at many different primary schools. As a development officer, he was able to work with and coach children, which gave him a valuable learning experience in his coaching development.

Wayne advocates the empowerment approach and the use of Game Sense with children (see Chapter Two), so that they can understand what they are doing and why. Children who become self-aware learn about the game and themselves as players. On the sideline, we always hear parents and coaches directing the children as to where to go and what to do. We take the decision making away from them. If we used an empowerment approach with children, they:

> ... will make better decisions and enjoy the experience more. If you can give kids lots of game specific activities, let them have fun, use a questioning approach so that you develop self-awareness, and empower them to be responsible for what they are doing in the game, you'll get a good response from them. They may not win, but they'll enjoy it and make gradual improvements.

A key feature of Wayne's approach is his idea that players need to enjoy themselves. Wayne has worked with Bruce Pinel, a PhD student from the University of Otago, to introduce enjoyment to players' quality profiles (profiles which are made in collaboration with each player). He describes this venture as 'a really good initiative ... it's an obvious challenge to professional sport'. Wayne feels that enjoyment is a major factor in coaching because if players do not enjoy the sport, they will give it less effort. Recognising that this enjoyment is a key to young children's participation as well, he says:

> The first thing to do is find out what they enjoy about their sport and make sure
> you are catering for those things. Do enjoyment profiles. Find out what they
> expect from you as a coach. Do they expect you to be a ranter and raver, or do
> they want you to give them fun activities? You need to know what they want …
> You have that one hour a week [to coach them]. You don't want to waste that
> hour so how you structure the training sessions will determine how much you
> all enjoy it.

On the development of rugby players in New Zealand and the importance of coaches learning to empower them, Wayne suggests:

> I'd like all rugby coaches in New Zealand to encourage greater player owner-
> ship of and responsibility for performance. Our players need to understand the
> game better. They need to be able to question their coaches and in turn be
> questioned. We need to influence young players more positively, instil values at
> a young age and encourage all-round skill development. Developing intelligence
> in players and ensuring they are more self-directed will bear huge rewards for
> New Zealand rugby in the future.

Some of the Challenges to Using Empowerment

Although, as Wayne's experience indicates, an empowerment approach
offers many advantages, it also brings challenges to coaches who wish to
make use of it. This section draws attention to some of those challenges,
along with Wayne's response to them.

A challenge indicated in both research and practice is that using an
empowerment approach is very time consuming. It takes time for athletes to become accustomed to being coached in a different way. It also
takes time to develop athletes into thinking athletes. Yet the long-term
advantages ultimately override this challenge, as athletes begin to make
informed decisions, have fun and increase their self-esteem. In line with
this idea, Wayne notes:

> It is going to take a while … and that's what people don't understand. If the
> quality outcome you are after is satisfaction, then we got that straight away. As I
> said the first year [of building the team culture, without actually winning the
> Super 12s] was exciting. Since then, we have won the tournament twice, but to
> me it's not the winning that counts—it's doing your best to win. Having fun and
> learning together is a rewarding experience. We've had hard times, but gener-
> ally the smile on their faces is the biggest indicator to success. Seeing a group of
> talented individuals selflessly giving to each other and enjoying the experience
> makes coaching worthwhile.

Another time constraint might be:

… one player who is struggling, the rest of team is going well and they want to keep the momentum up. Particularly if it is a Thursday night training, the last training before the game, you want flow, you want continuity, you want a bit of feeling being built up. If you step in and stop that through questioning one player or trying to get instructional, it is quite often negative. The hardest part about the art of coaching is understanding when they are on a roll, and when to step out.

Observation is a big part of empowerment as is getting the questions right. It is quite hard … One thing I found difficult earlier on was sitting back and observing for three or four minutes before coming in. When you are trying to establish yourself, you'll find a lot of young coaches feel like they've got to get in there to espouse their knowledge. They have got to show that they know what is right and what is wrong. Even when [the coach is] using a questioning approach, they feel they have to show that they are involved.

Another concern for the development of empowering coaches is the perception that a coach has to reel off all his or her knowledge to the players, when really coaching is about enabling them to learn.

Wayne was asked about any difference in success between a prescriptive (autocratic) coach and an empowering coach:

It depends whether you want long-term success or short-term success. A team that you hear in the changing room yelling and screaming as the coach gets them hyped up, are often beaten because they will only have short-term success against you (they are going to be really tough in the first 20 minutes). If you just ride it out and keep your cool, react to what you see, talk, guts it out and be relentless, you'll get on top of them every time. It is the same in a seasonal sense. The teams who are autocratically run have short-term success, do really well earlier on. Teams like ours tend to take awhile for everything to come together.

I know one of my faults is that early in the season I tend work on too many things. The players can sometimes get too cluttered, but I believe it's important to show improvements throughout the season. Whereas autocratic teams are really good earlier on, they tend to peter out a wee bit. In contrast, empowerment ensures a dynamic, living, learning environment. You've got new players coming in, new ideas, new intellectual capital, [and] new leaderships. It is ever changing and for that reason, long-term success is often sustainable.

As he explained above, Wayne is still learning about how to use an empowerment approach. Here, he describes some of the interesting learning processes that he went through when he introduced empowerment to the Canterbury Crusaders:

When I first came to the job (my first year working for the Crusaders was 1997), we didn't make the players follow our systems and processes rigidly. For example, with regard to individual game review systems, I said, 'Look this is what we'd like you do, but if you don't feel comfortable doing it, don't do it'. It is no longer the case. [The player has to] be able to sit down with me and go through the game. Effectively, players have to be able to identify what needs to be improved and how they are going to do it. Players have to schedule individual sessions in a weekly planner to ensure they fit in with team commitments. I want to see players organising other guys to help them get improvements. We like the players to go out and actually simulate the situation or skill they are trying to improve.

One of the mistakes I made when first using empowerment was to not explain what I was doing. This created unnecessary conflict at training. Instead of just giving an answer, players often tried to justify their actions. In my second year, I explained that we were using a questioning approach to develop self-awareness and tactical understanding, which was bought into by the players.

Wayne tells the story about when some players decided that they needed traditional coaching. Their concern drew Wayne's attention to the need for flexibility in coaching:

In 1998, we worked hard to make the players proud of the ownership they had about the way the team operated. We met often to ensure things were operating effectively. We established the game plans together, and the players were responsible for their own game reviews and debriefs. The players owned and understood every area of the game. The coaches facilitated these processes, provided guidance but became directive only when necessary. We laid the foundations, the players won the football games.

In 1999, we started the season the same way and it was going pretty well before we hit a trough. At one stage when we were playing the Stormers in Cape Town, we lost the game and dropped to eighth in the competition. Things weren't happening. We weren't playing the way we wanted to, we weren't effecting what we'd been doing in training.

Two senior players came to Steve and I that night and said, 'You have to lead us out of this. You are going to have to take control and show us the way'. It was an interesting response. They felt that things were being taken for granted by some of the players. They were getting a little bit sloppy and needed direction. It taught me that a coach must be flexible enough to provide what is required at the time. Sometimes all the players need is to be told what to do.

I didn't know at the time [of this challenge] because we'd been so successful in 1998. I just assumed that [empowerment] was the only model we should follow. It really showed that you have to be on your toes. Being a leader means you have to adapt to the team's needs at the time, and not let winning be your enemy by making you complacent. If there is incohesiveness in your team, you have a responsibility to sort it out. If you notice morale dropping, you must take decisive action before the situation becomes chronic.

Wayne describes his reaction to the players' concern and how ultimately the players too saw the advantage of the empowerment approach:

We didn't change the methodology … really. I think their point was, 'You make some of the hard calls that need to be made. Be definite about the way we are going to go forward in training and what our game requires …'. For a while, we became more instructional at trainings and more directive about how the game was to be played.

Another turning point for the team in 1999 was also in sending signals that no one is beyond being replaced in the team. Even though the next game (Northern Bulls) was the most crucial game of the season, we played Aaron Flynn at halfback and Leon MacDonald at first five. Regular stars Justin Marshall and Andrew Mehrtens were on the bench. It demonstrated to the team that we trusted everyone in the squad and expected every player to be up to the mark. We won the game and we went on to win the championship.

One further challenge in using an empowerment approach, Wayne indicates, may arise if the right team culture is not in place:

I can't see too many disadvantages to the approach, unless you haven't got the culture and you can't trust the players to be genuine about it. You need to have an honest team to get improvements.

Adapting the Approach to the All Blacks—Wayne's Plans

Wayne was asked about how he would implement this approach with the All Blacks. The time constraints were a major concern, but he was prepared to take on the challenge:

It is a concern in that we don't have a long lead-in period to our first game. However, this is the approach I am going to be using. I'll modify it, ensuring that I am being really clinical in the way I use questioning. I need to get to the guts of what I want to achieve … like planning the questions. [I need to plan] the activities and know what I am going to see, use questions to sort it out. Tony Gilbert (assistant coach) has a similar approach to me, a lot of experience and wisdom. I foresee us having a very good relationship.

What we are going to have to be careful with is that we don't give information overload with the players, a trap I fell into at times with the Crusaders. We had two and a half months [with the Crusaders] before we played and you can generate a lot of learning in that period. With the All Blacks, it will be really interesting. Tony and I are sowing the seed now with the public and with the players that we need to change. We can no longer play the traditional All Black game and be successful. If people agree that is what we have to do, then we are going to have to be given some time to do that. Instead of running over top of opponents, we have to learn to run into gaps, and develop the skill level to do that.

It is going to be a trade-off between learning that new approach, but doing it simply enough so that they perform straight away. Simplicity will be a key, culling out the peripheral stuff, so we can get quickly to the core of what needs to be done.

I think they will respond really well. There is so much intellectual capital in the All Blacks. They know the game. You can't be dumb in the All Black world, so I think we'll all enjoy it.

Conclusion

Although Wayne does not have all the answers and does not claim to be an expert, he provides coaches with some insight into how to implement an empowering approach. He has suggested that the players are intrinsically motivated and learn well when coaches use questioning and Game Sense to enhance decision making.

Learning the empowerment approach is not an easy task, but the benefits to the team and individual athletes are immense. The learning process is easier when coaches begin by considering how such an approach might be suitable for them and remembering that the process of implementation requires time. Coaches will make progress by trying new ideas and continuing to self-reflect on how the approach is working within the team. There are also techniques, such as questioning and understanding Game Sense, that need to be practised. The more coaches practise, the better they will be at ensuring athletes have ownership of their learning and direction of their sporting and life experiences.

References

Belasco, J.A., & Stayer, R.C. (1993). *Flight of the Buffalo: Soaring to Excellence, Learning to Let Employees Lead.* New York: Warner.

Landsberg, M. (1996). *The Tao of Coaching: Boost Your Effectiveness at Work by Inspiring and Developing Those Around You.* London: Harper Collins.

There is no point in coaching unless the teaching you do helps the student to overtake you.

—Rene Deleplace, mentor of Pierre Villepreux

Innovation is the one weapon that can't be defended against.

—Sun Tzu

Chapter Four

In every success story, you find some-
one has made a courageous decision.

—Peter F Drucker

Developing Junior Coaches: Case Studies of Hugh Galvan and Paul McKay

In this chapter, we follow a journey of two developing junior coaches who have decided that athletes learn best and gain more satisfaction when their coaches use an empowerment approach. These coaches discuss where and how they travelled with their coaching styles before empowerment. They highlight their reasons for adopting an empowering approach, their methods of empowering athletes and their challenges and concerns in implementing this approach, with thoughts for coaches about to embark on using an empowerment approach. Athletes of these two junior coaches also give their point of view of the empowerment approach.

The coaches interviewed come from different backgrounds, although both are past rugby players. The first coach is Hugh Galvan who, when interviewed, was coach of an under 14 school boy rugby team and had coached secondary school-aged children in various sports (mostly rugby) for six years. Hugh is a trained physical education teacher and is currently lecturing at a college of education in sport coaching and physical education. Paul McKay is a sport coaching student at a college of education. When interviewed, he had just completed a season as co-coach with Hugh. Paul has also coached an under 21 rugby team. The following is a synopsis of what Hugh and Paul said about their coaching in the interviews.

Philosophy on Coaching

Hugh and Paul differ somewhat in their coaching philosophies. However, they share the core beliefs of empowerment that the athlete is the central focus, is the decision maker and should take ownership for his or her learning and performance. Both coaches feel that they are still learning and developing their empowerment approach.

Hugh's philosophy is based partly on his background as a teacher. The concept of success underpins his philosophy:

Hugh: I believe my philosophy to be built around one word … success. If players are succeeding then chances are they are enjoying their rugby and are motivated to apply themselves. Success, to me, is observed in many forms and rugby provides the vehicle or the context to achieve success.

Having players improve their attitude towards school through their positive experience with rugby is success. Seeing players learn and develop skills necessary to relate to others in a team is success. Seeing them put into practice the aims that we have developed, as a team, and observing their physical skills improve are keys to success. Players [who] want to turn up to practice, enjoy what they are doing and are motivated to improve individually and collectively, is success.

As a coach, my challenge is to foster opportunities and experiences that achieve this success within a player-centred environment. If I am able to do this, then I believe we start to develop well-rounded individuals, not just players. I would like to think it is an 'holistic' coaching philosophy.

Hugh was asked how success and winning were related:

Hugh: … we (the team) tend to hold the belief that we focus our rugby on what we can influence—that is, performance goals—as opposed to outcome (winning) goals. We try not to worry about the outcome as we have little control over it. We generally can't determine how fast the opposition will run, how well they pass the ball, how well they will throw the ball in, etc. If we always used outcome goals as an emphasis and lost, we would be continual failures. Problems such as player motivation would then develop. Therefore, by using performance goals, we go out on the field to focus on doing what we do very well. If we achieve what we set out to do, then we are succeeding. Winning (outcome) becomes the secondary result of our performance goals.

Paul is at a point in constructing his coaching philosophy where he finds it quite difficult to put his ideas into concise words:

Paul: My philosophy now is an open-ended sentence. I have a philosophy, but it is open because I am adding to it constantly. It's really based around learning; learning how to be an effective coach and how I apply that learning to the athletes. I am learning how to be an effective coach, but the way that I apply that to my coaching changes, so it is flexible according to my athletes. As everyone is different, I am trying to contribute to each individual's learning. If I were to put my philosophy into one sentence, I would say that I am attempting to promote the holistic development of my athletes …

Paul, like Hugh, views the athlete as a whole person (see Chapter Seven), with rugby as only one part of that person's life:

Paul: Rugby isn't what I am trying to achieve; I am not trying to give them a greater ability in rugby alone. I am using rugby as a means to an end where we can, not mould, but develop people's physical skills, which may be important for them. I think it gives them good habits for life, through being physically active. Also in mental development through your questioning and empowerment they are developing their thinking a lot more, not only about rugby, but situations in how they can act around other people, how they treat others. That comes into the social part of it where we are developing their social skills, their acceptance of others and teamwork.

Hugh and Paul were asked if their philosophies have changed over time:

Hugh: [My philosophy of] success has certainly not changed, but the way I now attempt to achieve it has. In the past, I have been the sole decision maker who set standards, expectations, consequences and goals for individuals and the team. I coached this way because I often modelled my coaching style on how past coaches of mine had coached me. To me, I was reproducing a coaching style that reflected the status quo to coaching rugby. Now though, it is the coach and players who work together to achieve those same aims.

Paul: My philosophy has definitely changed over the past year-and-a-half. This is mainly due to the fact that I have attempted to adopt this Game Sense and empowerment technique. Also, through my degree at the college of education, I have developed a continuing self-awareness of my coaching and the constant self-reflection, which I believe is necessary to enhance my coaching effectiveness and identify my weaknesses. This is why I refer to my philosophy as being an open sentence because I am constantly developing it to suit both myself and my athletes.

Wayne Smith highlights his philosophy on player rotation (see Chapter Three). Hugh and Paul have a similar philosophy in that all players earn their right to be in the team and should have equal right to play:

Hugh: Paul and I had in our own minds the belief that we needed a player-rotation system as opposed to selecting the 'best' 15. We believed that the benefits would strengthen our team game, as players developed an awareness of the positional requirements of others around them and a greater self-belief in realising they had much to offer to the team.

The trick was to get players to want this as well. We put the consequences of each system to them. It certainly didn't take much for the players to select a rotation system. After all, when developing our team expectations at the start of the season, a common reason they gave for enjoying rugby was playing. Very quickly, the players realised that the coaches' idea of the best 15 may not reflect their own and as a result their season could be spent sitting on the bench, should they not make the starting team. For the system to work, we needed to develop players with the confidence and physical skills to play in more than one position.

A good example of player self-belief was when we made the final two years ago. We had injuries to several key players prior to the final. This had little disruption to our preparation as the players backed each other to fill any 'gaps'. In the final, we had further injuries. Players could be seen making minor positional changes themselves to account for those going on to the field. They backed themselves and those around them to carry out their job.

We do not aim to turn the players into 'jacks of all trades, but masters of none'! We simply believe it irresponsible to specialise a 14-year-old into one position, as the player may never have the same physical attributes after adolescence. By limiting the players to the one position, we believe they can be disadvantaged in their teens and beyond. The benefits of our rotation system are that combinations are developed, players can be relied upon when required to play at any time and each player realises he has a valuable contribution to make to the team's performance. Individual motivation to strive for the team is seen.

Many coaches say that all players have a valuable contribution to make to the team. However, they contradict themselves by keeping players on the sideline, often for several games at a time. How demotivating can that be to a player?

Paul: I think Wayne Smith tactically rotates during the game, whereas Hugh and I rotate at half time based on a roster system that we have. If you have the traditional starting 15 and a reserves bench who only come on when there is an injury, then the combination of skill is lost because the new player is unfamiliar playing with the rest of the starting line-up. There is also a question of team cohesion … there may be ill feeling between players of the starting 15 and the reserves, and a loss of enthusiasm [among] these reserves if they don't make the starting line-up.

The difference between Wayne's approach to rotation and ours is that we work out who has been playing a lot and who has not and attempt to give everyone equal game time. This is not performance-based and is merely done in equal participation … We put a lot of faith in our entire team and not just our starting 15. Obviously at under 14 level there are some huge differences in athletic ability, but if we had a star player who had potential to [help us] win the game, and was in the starting line-up, but it was his turn to rotate, then we would rotate him anyway. We [believe] equal participation is far more important than winning and we have confidence in the substitution of players to do their best.

The other great thing about the rotation system is that each player has the opportunity to learn the skills of two or three different positions, within reason. Obviously, we wouldn't put a halfback into the front row because of safety concerns. The players themselves are enthusiastic to do it too, because it increases their amount of game time if they are able to play in more than one position. From a coaching standpoint, this is very advantageous because then you have a team of utility players, who can cover every position if an injury occurs.

If teams are coached with a rotational system and player positional versatility approach then, if an injury occurs, ... it would be covered by another member of that team. Therefore the team cohesion would be greater than if an unfamiliar player was drafted in who didn't know any combinations, etc.

Process of Developing as a Coach

Both coaches say they followed a traditional style of coaching before they concluded that it was not the best way to practise their philosophies and started using an empowerment approach. In developing as a coach, it is not easy to fully engage in an empowering way given the prevalence of the traditional approach both now and previously when Hugh and Paul experienced coaching as players. Yet, despite their history as players (and as a coach in Hugh's case), they have fully immersed themselves in the empowering approach.

Hugh and Paul discuss the disadvantages of coaching with a prescriptive approach:

Hugh: ... in the past I will have coached in a style that I have learned from other coaches. Ultimately this was a prescriptive approach. I look back now and cringe at some of the things I did. Certainly, [I used to] be more directive, make a lot more decisions for players and didn't include them in decision-making processes, yet ironically, they play the game, not me ...

As a coach, I was simply loading players with information and sending them on their way. Many of them have great ideas, but as coaches, we tend to think we are the only source of information. Essentially, the prescriptive coaching style was 'programming' players to play the game. Unfortunately, this approach failed to fully equip players with the skills to think for themselves and make decisions in pressure situations. It gave quick-fix answers to problems, but stifled long-term learning.

I believe traditional sports, like rugby, now have to compete with many other alternative sports and activities that are meeting the needs of individuals in today's society. Now individuals are often wary of how they invest their time and effort. They want instant gratification for these efforts and lack perseverance for sticking with activities that are not meeting their needs. What we have always done, as coaches, isn't working because if it was, we wouldn't have increased drop-out rates from rugby. We need to assess how we are coaching and make the necessary changes to meet the needs of today's players.

I think empowerment begins to achieve this. Written feedback from the players [see later section in this chapter] at the end of the year tells us it is so and to me this is important. In the past, I would have said, 'This is what we are doing, this is how we are going about it'. While using the traditional approach to coaching, I thought I had motivated players. Looking back now, I think that quite possibly, many were simply compliant. There is a big difference. I am far more comfortable with how I am going about coaching now because I think it is starting to meet the needs of the individual players. I think if we can do that, we can contribute to rugby well beyond an 80-minute game.

Paul: In rugby, I think the biggest problem with traditional coaches these days is that they are only looking for athletic ability and they are only looking to develop athletic ability. Last year, I was like that when I took an under 21 team. I was a traditional coach and it didn't work. They learned nothing basically …

[Traditionally] athletes aren't given the opportunity to form their own ideas. Information is pumped into them and they just listen to what they have to do. However, with the Game Sense and empowerment approach, the athletes try new things under the guidance of the coaches until they can find things that work well for them. The coach is there to give some ideas and knowledge and then the individual chooses which ideas work best for them. If the athlete is forming ideas for him or herself, then there is a high chance that they will remember it. If the information is thrown at the athlete, then they may have difficulty remembering it.

As suggested in Chapter One and reinforced in the coaches' statements, empowerment is an approach that will help develop athletes holistically (i.e. physically, psychologically and socially) and 'empower' them to take responsibility for their own learning. Hugh and Paul were asked who or what had been influential in their development as an empowering coach:

Hugh: As a coach, I am continuously learning. I have no doubts that this will ever change. While we ultimately determine our own destiny, there have been many experiences, events and people that have contributed to my development. They have been influential, ultimately, because I am keen to learn and prepared to change.

It has certainly been the work of Wayne Smith, his coaching staff and the Canterbury Crusaders environment that really enticed me to delve further into empowerment. I was interested in the Crusaders and how they could create what appeared to be a fantastic environment on and off the field.

Past coaches I have had and players have influenced me too. At times, bad experiences with past coaches have motivated me not to be like them. Books, videos, coach education courses and discussions with other coaches have all been an influence.

Paul: … when I was in the [sport coaching] course, through [a lecturer] and Hugh mainly. In the course, [empowerment and Game Sense] got touched on in the first year, not forced down our throat, which was really good. At the start, I thought, 'I haven't been taught this, it is not right. It's too soft and filled with emotions.' It took me a long time to recognise it but, slowly, we looked at Game Sense a lot deeper.

I did a bit of self-reflection of my coaching and, through videos and practical examples of how Game Sense worked, I thought, 'Hey, this is contributing to the learning of the athletes rather than the coach being an instructor'. You are helping them develop.

What I basically did was that I looked at some of the outcomes that Game Sense coaching had had, Wayne Smith was a big one. Even lower than that, the lecturers were doing it at the [college of education]. It seemed that quite a few people started using it. I ended up doing a bit of personal research about it and looked at Game Sense. [Others] looked more at empowerment as well, questioning and feedback. Then, I tried it at the end of last year and I found that it worked really well. I had a lot more attention from the athletes and at the end of the session, they had learned a lot more and could actually recall what we were talking about and doing.

Hugh and Paul acknowledge that as developing coaches, their use of questioning as a coaching technique is crucial to getting athletes to think for themselves:

Hugh: Questioning is a part of the approach that is vital. [It] can be challenging because as coaches we are often tempted to automatically give players the answers. It is really important to resist this temptation. Players need to feel comfortable in that they can contribute in some way with an answer and yet not feel inferior or put down. I had always used questions to some degree as a coach in the past. However, the questions were too closed and failed to fully engage players in learning by having them think for themselves.

[Effective questioning] is certainly the ability to give players the time to process the question and come up with an answer. You need patience as a coach. There is often a predetermined answer in your mind. The skill is to reach this by directing open-ended questions, such as how, what, why or where, to players. At times the players are unsure of a response or [are] moving in a direction with their answers that you do not want. The trick is for you to rephrase questions, use probes or present a different scenario for players to achieve your goal. You learn a great deal about how players think, what they know, their understanding of the game and reasons behind the options they chose in game situations. Effective questioning is an art. To succeed at it, a coach must be prepared to persevere and practise questioning.

Paul: [When questioning] you are saying 'How do we do this?' and you already know what you want from the athletes, but you are questioning them about it, so that when they do come up with the answers, they feel as though they have accomplished something by thinking of the solution for themselves. I think that is how we plan our trainings as well. We, as coaches, know what we want to achieve at practice (usually based on the previous Saturday or the previous training). However, we go to practice and … question the team about what they want to achieve and usually they come up with the same ideas that we have already planned. The technique that is [an] integral [part of] enticing their ideas is that of questioning.

[To help in planning,] we ask questions and then try to manipulate their answers through probing in an attempt to get them to say what we want. If this doesn't happen and they have different and valid ideas, we will try and incorporate their ideas as much as we can without disrupting our plan too much. I think that flexibility is an important aspect of coaching. However if you let the players run the entire session, then it can destroy the purpose of the practice. That is where the questioning and manipulation comes in. You have to base your questions around what you want them to say and then probe for the appropriate answers.

Hugh and Paul describe how they learned about developing and asking meaningful questions:

Hugh: Reading books and articles, discussions with other people and watching other coaches question their players, videoing yourself coaching and reflecting on your performance, are great ways to assess your questioning skills. Learning by trial and error is paramount to improving questioning skills. It is important to persevere and be prepared to make mistakes in order to learn. Ironically, you learn a lot about your ability to develop meaningful questions from the players' answers. A blank look on a player's face lets you know your questions need work.

Paul: Questioning is a really difficult thing to do. You actually have to know a lot of answers and you've got to know how to aim your questioning to get the answer. That is where the manipulation comes in. You've got the answer but you try to manipulate your questions so that they come up with the answers (probing). You have to be really careful not to give them the answer because it is very tempting to do. If you ask a question, 'How are you going to get past those defenders?' and they don't come up with your answers, it is sometimes very easy to just give them the answer. Sometimes it gets to the point where you say, 'How do you get past that player, do we kick or pass in this situation?' You are giving them two options.

The coaches were also asked about how they have learned to self-

analyse their coaching (see Chapter Ten for further discussion of this tech-nique):

Hugh: There are several sources of information that have helped me in this process. Reflecting on the sessions, and identifying what you believe are to be strengths and weaknesses to the session, is important. It enables you to build on the strengths and eliminate weaknesses. Watching yourself on video helps this process. It can be scary at first. Videos do not lie.

Working with another coach or having a mate give feedback after watching you coach is valuable. Paul and I have had many discussions on aspects of our coaching. His feedback is great.

Players too are very perceptive of your coaching. Watching how they are reacting at training tells you a great deal about your coaching. Getting direct answers from them is another approach. We did this in conversation with play-ers and with a written evaluation. Their comments were very interesting and assisted our coaching immensely.

Being honest with yourself is critical to effective self-analysis. You will struggle with the approach without the ability to ask honest questions of your perfor-mance and act on the feedback.

Paul: Self-reflection. I look at the ways that I apply my coaching and see if it is effective or not and then after the session, I self-reflect back and [might] say, 'Should I have pointed out this kid in front of everyone when he was doing something wrong? What effect did I have on him?' I might think that it wasn't very good, so the next time I'll make an effort to not pinpoint individuals.

Another part of self-reflection is feedback from another coach, like Hugh. He gave me a lot of feedback, so that is a form of self-reflection. He can tell you what you did and you can look back and say, 'Maybe it wasn't that effective'.

Another part to self-reflection is reading your athletes (Hugh terms this 'with-it-ness'): how did they react to what they were doing, were they enthusiastic or were they bored? You can reflect even as you are doing it. You might say, 'That didn't work', so you make sure you don't do it again, or 'That worked really well, I might try that again'.

In developing empowerment as an approach, Hugh and Paul admit they must constantly research and seek ways to learn about such an ap-proach. Each of them had different ways of developing their approach, but for both the key was seeking information by reading, asking ques-tions and learning from advice:

Hugh: To me, the essence to achieving success with the approach is having the hunger to learn. If you lack this zest, I believe you will struggle to progress. Reading books, talking with people and sharing ideas, attending coaching courses, being prepared to acknowledge we make mistakes—but learning from them, watching videos, it all helps. However, all of this is fruitless if you are not prepared to be open-minded. If you 'take the blinkers off' and absorb information, but sift through it and decide what works best for you and your specific coaching situation, then I think you're on the way forward.

Paul: ... I wanted to learn about Game Sense and empowerment and hopefully change a few coaching styles of different coaches, or traditional coaches. I was really enthusiastic about it. Then my enthusiasm became a bit of an obsession. [I started] reading Game Sense books, articles, everything, asking a lot of coaches about games that they do, empowerment, questioning, like the work that we did in class. All of this became a bible for me. I read over those resources before every session.

Using Game Sense as Part of the Empowerment Approach

As is evident from some of their comments, Hugh and Paul are advocates of Game Sense (see Chapter Two) and they are keen to apply it to their trainings. They find the approach has many advantages and comment on the success of using it:

Hugh: Ask coaches about the qualities they'd like to have in athletes at the highest level and I'm sure they'll use words such as good decision makers, [being] motivated, physically fit and skilful, quick thinkers, ability to cope with pressure, [and] tactically aware players. I pose the question that if we want our very best athletes to possess such qualities, why not start with our young players?

In my experience, the use of Game Sense develops these qualities. Having players train within the context of a rugby game as encouraged through Game Sense is so beneficial to their understanding and performance of the game. At times, the players' progress over a season is quite amazing to observe. Generally, rugby players are involved in the game because they enjoy playing it. Game Sense enables this 'play' quality to be fostered and, as a result, motivation increases. Players love it.

However, the essence of Game Sense is more sophisticated than just playing games. It is a coaching approach that uses well-defined progressions of game-like activities that have a clear purpose in mind. For example, the game may be based on eliminating your weaknesses or exploiting those of the opposition. You only have to see some of the feedback from players, to gain an understanding of the value of Game Sense.

Paul: You can present a situation, a game situation, and say 'Your goal is to get a try, how can you do that?' Then players must think of ways to get past other players to achieve that goal. Scoring a try is the outcome and the players must think of ways to achieve that outcome. This includes them trying different things, discussing among themselves and also [getting] a small amount of feedback from the coaches. I think that as a coach, I have learned a lot more from my players than I have taught them. I think that this empowerment approach involves a manipulation of ideas, bringing out athletes' ideas, so that they can achieve their goals.

[If] a coach was to come to me, I would say, keep your traditional outlook for now, but try to incorporate aspects of Game Sense slowly so you can work up to the whole approach. You are not doing yourself any justice by trying to say, 'I want to be a game-centred coach, full stop'. You can't do that.

An example was [when] Hugh said to me, 'What can we do for our warm-up?' It's really hard, as a Game Sense coach, to think of games, original games that players are not going to get bored [with]. I said to Hugh that I couldn't think of any games, and [asked him] what to do. He ended up saying, 'Look why don't you do grids?' I said, 'But that is not Game Sense, there is no opposition.' He said, 'It doesn't matter, it is a warm-up and you don't have to have games for everything. If you can't think of a game, then don't do a game, but try to do games for the majority of your session.' If you haven't got an idea, don't worry about it too much. Concentrate on what you do well.

Advantages to an Empowerment Approach

Hugh and Paul were asked what advantages they perceive in an empowerment approach:

Hugh: Player motivation is an obvious advantage. Players are enjoying their rugby. As a result, the team climate is very strong. In addition, the approach tends to produce players with a greater appreciation for the game, who are more disciplined and take greater responsibility for their actions. Providing more choice and control for players is important in empowering players.

You must remember that the process is more complex than simply saying to players, 'Go do everything'. In fact, I disagree with people who say empowerment is flowery, that the players will run the 'whole ship' and the approach doesn't reinforce discipline. As a coach, you are the 'captain' of the ship. However, unlike an autocratic coach, we do not flog our crew to make the boat go forward. The skill is to develop a self-motivated, well disciplined, keen and eager crew who are prepared to go beyond the call of duty because they *respect* you, not because they are made to. I've found discipline is more effective with an empowering approach. It is amazing the expectations that players put on themselves and the consequences they're prepared to operate by as long as you, as the coach, are prepared to be consistent and carry out these consequences.

For example, early on in the season, one of our best players didn't ring us when he wasn't going to be at training. In developing our team expectations, players had said that such incidents should mean the players didn't take the field ahead of others. We carried this out and the player was a reserve. Everyone expected this to happen and appreciated it when it did happen. Team cohesion was certainly enhanced.

Paul: The benefits of empowerment and Game Sense are sometimes difficult to identify until you have been using it for some time, especially when you are just beginning to use this approach. It is difficult to see the learning retention that occurs until it becomes autonomous to the athletes, usually later in the season.

In our coaching this year, Hugh and I focused on introducing these new concepts to our athletes and slowly increased the amount of questioning etc., that we did with them. During the last half of our season, we have really seen the team's development in terms of their learning and performance—not just winning but, more importantly, achieving their goals. Just after their term holidays, the team played without a training session and it looked as though they had forgotten everything that they had learned. But, we re-emphasised some of the things that we had practised during the season and in the next few sessions with them, they remembered it all. Then after these few sessions, their development came in leaps and bounds and they really hit their peak and continued their performance for the rest of the season.

With the approach, we have set an initial base of learning, and our peak has come a bit later than other teams, but we have peaked for longer, which separates us from other teams who have peaked early but dropped their performance late in the season.

The Process of Empowering Players

Obviously, with an empowerment approach, the focus is on empowering athletes. Hugh and Paul discuss their ways of achieving this goal and in so doing re-emphasise their philosophy of developing holistic athletes:

Hugh: There were a variety of ways to empower our rugby players. Establishing our beliefs, values, expectations and consequences were examples.

What we did this year was we asked three simple questions. The first was 'What do [you] enjoy about rugby?' The players came up with answers such as being part of the team, running with the ball, tackling, scoring tries and meeting people.

The next question was, 'What do you need to do to achieve these things?' The players identified responses such as be committed to self-practice and teammates, turn up to training on time, be a good listener.

The last question we asked was 'What do you think should happen if these things don't happen?' Essentially, these were the consequences for not meeting the expectations. The players expected these to be carried out by us. One of their answers was for players who did not meet expectations to go on the field ahead of others. Paul and I had our own expectations and consequences that we wanted the players to buy in to. The trick was to use probing questions or 'manipulate' their answers to achieve these ideas.

Another example is that we empowered players to come up with tactics and options to our game. For example, the forwards were given the problem of developing lineout options together. They came up with several possibilities, then [we went] through and tried them to decide which were the best. As a coach, I too will have had thoughts about options and moves (as a coach, this is still very important).

Within this process, we started out with very simple problems to solve. For example, the first instructions to those young players were, 'You need to set a lineout up so you can best win the ball'. Traditionally, the locks jump for the ball. In our particular case we had one of the biggest players in lock who was going to cause problems to the lifters because of his size. Initially, the players shuffled themselves into positions with the big lock being lifted. That is obviously what they'd always done. It wasn't working, so I went back to them with the same question again, 'You need to structure your lineout in a way that you can win the ball'. The players started to click on and they started shuffling people around, so lighter players were being lifted.

It takes time, but the trade-off is immense. For example, in the game, I have seen the players reorganise at lineout time to accommodate substitutions or lineout options that weren't working. To me this is a reflection of young players who are empowered. They are thinkers who can adjust to situations in their game. It does not happen by chance.

The use of Game Sense activities and meaningful questions, as previously discussed, is an important aspect of the empowerment process too. As coaches the key in the empowering of players is to know where you want to go. You still need your goals, knowledge of the game, direction and purpose. However, unlike the autocratic coach, the means to achieving the end is considerably different.

Paul: At the beginning, it didn't really hit them well because their traditional coaches told them everything—the drill, running, sprinting, going down on the ground, doing push-ups, all of that. Then we started (mostly Hugh) doing the Game Sense. It was good because he explained the importance of doing it, but still they were a bit sceptical. They would say, 'I think we should be running and doing push-ups'.

I think at one stage, one of the players was injured and we asked him to take a warm-up. He decided on downs and ups: 'We'll sprint, dive on the ground, get up and sprint, dive on the ground'. This is what their former traditional coaches have taught them. However, what is the importance of this type of activity? Sure, they may be getting fit, but is it specific to a game situation with opposition?

Games can actually be fitness-oriented at the same time as being fun. The players also learn a lot out of real game situations. I think they really learned a lot, but it took a lot of getting used to as a coach with this new approach, let alone an athlete.

The players think it is second nature now. They are really willing to ask, answer and discuss questions. We always have a couple of people who are firing questions back at us and also answering questions. You can tell they are really thinking.

Players' Feedback to these Empowering Coaches

As part of their feedback process, Hugh and Paul asked the players to write evaluations of the various parts of the season. One of the first questions was, 'What did you learn this year?' Here is a sample of the typical answers:

- · 'I learned about having a positive attitude and playing as one unit.'
- · 'I learned how to play some new positions, e.g. flanker, and extend my ball handling skills all over the rugby field.'
- · 'How to play in unfamiliar positions.'
- · 'That you can win by not putting on your best team.'
- · 'Play as a team, work together, have fun.'

The next question that related to empowering was, 'What was the team spirit like at the end of the year?' Typical answers were:

- · 'We had come on a long way and ended up playing with just the one goal and started playing together.'
- · 'We were positive and played more as one unit.'
- · 'It was good fun playing with cool team and cool coaches.'
- · 'Everyone was enjoying themselves.'
- · 'All working together and helping each other. Played good rugby because of this.'

Aware that the players were unaccustomed to this empowerment approach, Hugh and Paul were interested to determine their reaction to their questioning technique. For the evaluation they asked, 'We used lots of questions to help you learn. Explain how you felt when we asked you questions at the start of the year.' Responses included:

- · 'I felt quite good because you were getting to know about people and the team.'

- · 'Self conscious, was wondering what to say.'
- · 'Alright, I was normally unsure of the answer.'
- · 'It was a different way of coaching.'
- · 'Worried.'
- · 'Puzzled often.'
- · 'Good because it would put you in a situation and you had to tell what you would have done.'
- · 'Didn't know a lot of the answers.'

The players were then asked how they felt about the questioning by the end of the year:

- · 'I realised that you weren't trying to put us down so I would an-swer more freely.'
- · 'Still good because a person can never stop learning, no matter what age they are.'
- · 'I felt that it would make you think about things', 'More relaxed, did not worry me as much.'
- · 'I felt if I said the wrong thing, people wouldn't worry or put me down.'
- · 'It was good that we were asked what we thought of the team's position.'
- · 'More experienced.'
- · 'There was no right or wrong to the questions.'
- · 'Good, because it helped me with my game.'
- · 'Was able to answer a lot of the questions.'

As some of these answers show, the year involved some development for the athletes. If athletes are not used to being questioned, initially it is quite daunting. Once they realise the purpose of questioning and see its value, they seem to open up and feel that they are part of the decision-making process. Some of the feelings these players expressed relate to some strengths of the approach that Daryl Gibson and Anna Veronese discuss in Chapter Six.

Game Sense also featured in the evaluation. The players were asked, 'We tried to use lots of games and game-like activities to help you learn (e.g. attackers versus defenders). Did you like this method of coaching?

Explain why or why not.' The answers were enlightening, reflecting many of the advantages that Rod Thorpe linked with Game Sense (see Chapter Two):

· 'Yes, because it was used in actual matches. It also helped us develop moves, e.g. cuts.'

· 'Yes, I did because they got us ready for the game, and [taught] us what to do in game-like situations.'

· 'Yes, I thought it helped a range of skills with a range of games, e.g. kicking games, running attack, defence, etc.'

· 'Yes, I thought it was a good idea because it was more like playing a game, so we were ready come Saturday.'

· 'Yes, because what we did would help us out in the game, and teach us more.'

· 'Yes, it helped us to reflect what was happening at training to what was going on in the games.'

· 'Yes!! It improved our skills more than just doing drills, it was a more realistic environment.'

· 'Yes, because it was like a game, plus it was fun.'

· 'Yes, because it was like a game and it wasn't just boring running and tackling.'

· 'Yes, it is better than running up and down the field and we learn stuff at the same time.'

· 'Yes [I] did like this because it helped us in games and developed our skills'

· 'I did because it was like a game but we didn't do enough fitness.'

· 'I like it when we had game situations and there was live defence.'

· 'Yes I liked it better than running up and down the field to try and get fit with these attackers verse [defenders] it develop new skills.'

Interestingly, Hugh and Paul asked the athletes what they thought about setting their own goals—in other words, the experience of being empowered to decide the direction of the team and their season. The answers were also positive:

· '… it made it fair for the whole team.'

· '… then we would know what was to be expected of us, and we knew the consequences.'

· 'we found out exactly what we wanted out of this team and we worked towards them.'

· 'It was a good idea because we knew as a team our goals and if someone did not turn up to training, they knew they had done wrong and were going to be benched.'

· 'It was something the whole team agreed on and we can try to get those goals like playing as a team.'

· '… we set the rules and the consequences so it was fair to the whole team.'

· '… if we didn't have the goals or expectations we wouldn't have performed as well together (we were all working for the same goal).'

· '… it gave us something to work for.'

· '… everyone would be at the same level as everyone else.'

· '… we had to stick to those decisions if we liked it or not.'

· '… then we all wanted goals for ourselves and the team felt we needed towards the team.'

· 'It was a good idea. It gave us something to aim for at the end of the season.'

· 'We should have a say on how the team is run.'

In the written evaluation, Hugh and Paul asked about the player-rotation system: 'We used a rotation system to try and give players game time and develop skills of all 21 players. Was this a good idea? Why or why not?' Players offered these responses:

· 'Yes, everybody got a turn on the field and there were no grudges held in the team.'

· 'Yes and no, because I think everyone needs to have a game, because it is a whole team effort, but it can be boring standing on the sideline.'

· 'I think we should have players playing in their no. 1 position and people only fill in if they can't play.'

· 'Yes, no one was left out and our goal was to play as one unit and one unit is all getting game time.'

· 'Yes, then everyone felt that they were a part of the team and had lots of fun.'

· 'This was a good idea because everyone got even amounts of game time and knew that they had put in their best effort.'

· 'Yes!! It means that those that aren't able to make a starting 15 the opportunity to develop their skills.'

- 'Yes and no. It gives everyone a go, but we should have had a starting 15 each week and other players come on at half time.'

- 'Yes because everyone got game time.'

- 'Yes because then everyone played and it wasn't just the good players that played.'

- 'Yes, you can't leave 6 players on the sideline the whole game because they'll more than likely leave the team.'

- 'No because I think we should run with our best 15.'

- 'Yes, because when we had injuries, other players could come up.'

- 'Yes because we all got about the same game time so it was fair.'

- 'It was a good idea because everyone is playing rugby to get game time.'

- 'Yes it was because you know you will get a game and not 10 minutes at the end.'

As the above responses indicate, although some players opposed the rotation system, most were in favour and those opposed still saw the benefits of counting on the contribution of everyone in the team.

Finally, players commented on their experience of being able to play in several positions, in response to this evaluation question: 'We tried to build confidence in you to play more than one position. Do you think this was a good idea? Why or why not?'

- 'Yes and No, because it might help us when we are older but our performances this year, might have been worse than they could have been.'

- 'Yes, it is because you can now be versatile which will make you get into rep teams and other rugby teams.'

- 'Yes, it gave us a range of skills.'

- 'Yes, because you are not going to play one position all your life.'

- 'Yes, because I was not confident playing hooker at the start of the year, but now I love it and am confident to play any where.'

- 'Yes, we might find a position that we have never played before and enjoyed playing there.'

- 'Yes, I now have options to play in different positions next season— it also gave the forwards a better chance of getting a full game.'

- 'Yes, because if you want to get into teams, you need to play in more than one position.'

- 'Yes because when someone was away, someone could play in that position.'

- 'Yes, to help develop us as players.'

- 'Yes, because then you have more opportunities.'

- 'Yes because in the future it gives you more playing positions.'

- 'Yes because coaches like players who can play more than positions in case there is an injury.'

- 'Good idea because it will help us when we are playing in higher grades.'

Hugh and Paul found these written evaluations very valuable in analysing the season and their coaching. As they had really focused on the process of empowerment this season, the player evaluations gave them a sense of how the players responded to the empowerment approach, which, to many players, was a new style of coaching. The results of the evaluations reinforced their belief in empowerment as a tool that enables athletes to learn.

Some Challenges to Using Empowerment

Hugh and Paul were asked to relate some of the challenges they have faced in implementing empowerment with their teams, and how they have dealt with those challenges:

Hugh: We had to battle initially with [our introduction of] the [empowerment] approach. Some of the difficulties we faced were things like time, parents, the players (all of whom were new to the approach)—players who, at times, were taken [a]back by not being told what to do.

In the past, and this is one of the things we've changed, I decided to get through lineouts, scrums and rucking in the one session, for example. The answer to achieve all of this was to use a direct approach, which is the traditional coaching approach. However, with empowerment it is more time-consuming because learning is achieved through providing players with lots of problem-solving activities. The end result is that it takes longer to achieve because the coach is now guiding players to discover the answer.

You might get to training with a plan of what to work on, but because we are restricted with time, as we have boys that have to catch the bus, we have to modify activities a great deal. We need to be flexible and realise that you can't always get through the same amount of content as we'd want to. However, the positives, such as player motivation, understanding of the game and long-term learning, far outweigh the negatives.

Small steps are a key to the empowerment approach. This is particularly important if the players are new to empowerment or the coach is trying this approach for the first time. It can be daunting for players and coaches who are stepping outside their comfort zones in this respect. The importance of communicating to players what you are attempting to achieve is necessary. They will wonder what hit them if they are used to an autocratic coach and you suddenly start involving them in discussions, asking questions and so on. The challenge as a coach is to resist using a quick-fix answer from you to solve the immediate problem. For empowerment to succeed with a team with two coaches, you need coaches who are advocates of the approach. Paul has been great in this respect. He is keen, approachable and motivated to use the player-centred approach to coaching.

Paul: I really stabbed myself in the foot because I didn't take this approach one step at a time. I don't think it did me any good to go from a traditional coach through blatantly throwing information at my athletes to [a] full-on, game-centred empowerment approach. My coaching really took a step backwards. It has only just been developing lately because I now realise that I can't become a great Game Sense coach overnight. That is what I tried to do. I thought that it was an easy process, it's only games and a few questions, but it is not.

You can't attempt to research alone and think that you will develop. You have to have a plan on how you are going to do it. As I did in the first session, I concentrated on two things and that was games and questioning. That's what I think is important, that you have to concentrate on a few things at a time. The first session you may try games and then questioning and then three or four weeks later, or a month later, you can do another step to it. But I tried it all at once and that is why ... I failed. After I took a step back, I thought, 'No I am not going to do it any more'. It was too daunting. 'I stuffed it up, I can't go back to it.'

Then Hugh approached me and said, 'I need a coach, a coach for the backs. Do you think you could come and help me out?' I was a bit reluctant because I knew he was a game-centred coach and I knew that he was good and that I was a traditional coach, so I thought that there would be a clash. But Hugh was great. He said, 'I've got a lot to learn and I could learn a lot off of you and hopefully, you can learn a bit off of me as well.'

Just watching his coaching was amazing. The rapport that he has with the kids and the amount of learning that went on in the session is just incredible. This is the difference between the empowerment approach and the traditional approach. With empowerment, the athletes have a contribution to the team environment and actually want to be at training. However, with the traditional approach, it is very similar to the old saying, 'You can beat a dog and make him stay, but it's fear, not respect'.

Hugh was asked to elaborate on the issue of parents who are unconvinced that this empowerment approach is going to be effective for their

children:

> For many parents, the approach goes against what they understand as being the way to coach rugby. I believe they expect you should be seen 'coaching' players—that is, shouting orders and telling people what to do at practice and from the sideline. This absence of 'sideline coaching' is often difficult for some parents to accept, as they too can often become 'coaches' on Saturday. More often than not, this 'support' develops into the 'ugly parent' syndrome which the players dislike and we feel is quite unproductive. Having vocal parental support is fantastic. We had some of the best. However, there is a line between support and unhelpful comments.

> This year, we tried a different approach right from the start of the season. We kept parents well informed and reinforced to them the importance of open communication between parents and coaches. We sent a newsletter home to parents outlining to them what our beliefs and philosophies were as coaches. We included in that letter the three questions that we put to the players [see above, The Process of Empowering Players], so that they had a clear view of what the players liked about rugby and team expectations and consequences that had been established. We brought the parents together on the very first day for a meeting and reinforced to them what we were trying to achieve, that it may not be what they are used to, but this was what the players and coaches believe was going to be most beneficial for the team.

> Parents became very supportive and said positive things at our briefings during the season. We continually reinforced that it was great to see them being so positive. In essence, we were changing negative behaviours by reinforcing the positives and communicating to them. We were manipulating them in a positive way to suit the needs of our team. For example, a parent was standing next to us one day and he started to shout out something very unconstructive to his son and the team. He then restrained himself saying, 'Oh, I'd better not say that because that is not very positive'. We also saw a big change in that he started to ring us to say that his son wasn't at practice.

> I believe the example you set as a coach, to the parents, will very much influence how they react towards the players when they are on the sideline. Parents and players strongly indicated how pleased they were with the positive team support and atmosphere that was established throughout the year.

Some Advice for Coaches

As this approach was somewhat new to these coaches, they have offered some advice to those that are keen to try such an approach. Hugh and Paul wanted to highlight some suggestions to help coaches develop such an approach:

> **Hugh:** Firstly, I believe it is important for you to have a clear philosophy on coaching. You need to know why you are coaching and what you're aiming to

achieve. If you strongly believe something is worthwhile, then I suggest you will do all you can to achieve it. Increasing your knowledge of empowerment is important at this stage. This may be as a result of reading, watching empowering coaches coach or discussions with others. You need to be open minded, receptive to feedback and keen to learn. Putting your ego aside as a coach and acknowledging the contributions of others (this includes players) can be difficult for some, but it is important in this process.

Small steps towards empowerment are important. Do the simple things well and your confidence grows. For example, you may simply start attempting to use Game Sense activities with meaningful questions as part of warm-up routines. Communicate your intentions to players, parents and the like. You need them moving with you, not against you. Most people are reasonable if they know what you are aiming to achieve. Finally, be prepared to make mistakes. It is a natural part of the learning process. Change will not happen immediately, so you need to persevere.

Paul: You've really got to take the whole element of the self-reflection, reading your athletes, developing your ability to see their reactions. The way that they react, you will know straight away whether it has worked or if it hasn't worked. [It is important to be] able to put your ego aside and say to someone else, 'Please give me a hand. What have I done well and what do I need to improve on?'

A lot of people can't take a bit of criticism. It doesn't have to be negative, it could be constructive: 'Instead of doing this, why don't you try this one next time?' You have to be open to ideas from other people. It doesn't have to be coaches, it could be one of your friends on the sideline. So the athletes, other people's feedback, and research, all together are all great ways to learn about coaching and yes, we will always be learning.

You might read a book on Game Sense so you have some ideas on how to do new games. You can actually read a lot of different people's beliefs on Game Sense and empowerment and form your own ideas. That is what Hugh has done, he has his individual approach and it'll differ from Wayne Smith, it will differ from you. Even Rod Thorpe, when he came to New Zealand, had a different approach. Generally, they have the same principles, but some individuals have developed it more.

Another one is really trying it out. Don't be afraid to experiment because how do you know how it works, until you put it into action? You can get all the information you like, but if you don't practise it, you are not going to get the confidence to use it and you're not going to know how the players react. If you are doing research, the whole self-reflection comes into it. There are so many aspects to it. It is a lot of learning. That is why it is so daunting because there is all this new information to process, I am still daunted by it now (after a year of doing it). Perseverance is the key.

Conclusion

Hugh and Paul have highlighted the advantages and challenges to empowerment. They both stress that just attempting the approach is the first major hurdle. By giving it a go, then continuing to develop through self-analysis and evaluation, coaches will enable athletes to learn and provide them with internal motivation and enjoyment. Just remember to take one step at a time—advice similar to an idea you might pass on to your athletes.

Failure is never final and success is never-ending. Success is a journey, not a destination.

—Robert Schuller

When your values are clear to you, making decisions becomes easier.

—Roy Disney, US acress, author

Chapter Five

It is not only by the questions we have answered that progress may be measured, but also by those we are still asking.

—*Freda Adler, US educator, criminal justice specialist*

Applying Empowerment in Coaching: Some Considerations

Robyn Jones, University of Otago

My introduction to the empowerment philosophy came from a search to improve the decision making of football players during games. The ability to make appropriate decisions is an acknowledged characteristic of capable performers (Rink, French & Tjeerdsma, 1996). Having coached football professionally in the United Kingdom and the United States, I felt this aspect of players' performances always could, and should, be worked upon and improved. Indeed, decision-making ability is considered particularly important within a free-flowing dynamic sport such as football, in which the coach has limited influence once the game begins.

The coach's limited influence is also evident in rugby, hockey and netball, where players must be able to think on their feet and make appropriate decisions based on the needs of the situation they face. Generally, therefore, I wanted players to take greater responsibility for their own performances, particularly in changing strategies and tactics mid-game as the circumstance demanded. Rather than abandoning the agreed game plan, their decisions would amend it with reference to the corresponding strengths and weaknesses of the opposition. I wanted to develop in players an ability to assess the performance of themselves and their team during a game and make conscious decisions to improve this performance through considered tactical adjustments. To develop such decision-making abilities, they needed to become active learners, as when athletes and players seek their own solutions, learning is enhanced (Butler, 1997). In this respect, an empowerment philosophy seemed to answer my needs.

However, in 'buying in' to athlete empowerment as a concept I soon became aware of a trap that bedevils coach education—that is, the trap of prescribing action. I was tempted to believe that my adoption of an empowerment approach, or any other approach for that matter, was the only action that was needed to solve all my coaching woes. Elsewhere I have criticised such a simplistic view of coaching and related coach education programmes by arguing that, despite claims of its uniqueness as an occupation that combines many roles, to date coaching has been presented as a series of 'easy to follow' steps and strategies based on unconnected scientific lines (Jones, in press). According to this approach coaching is simple and unproblematic, and coaches are mere technicians who transfer unquestioned, prescribed knowledge.

This portrayal of a coach as one who only dominates and prescribes (Usher, 1998) is unacceptably one-dimensional. In reality, much of a coach's work is linked to a wide range of significant others (athletes, managers, parents, colleagues etc.) in a particular social situation (Jones & Armour, under review). Consequently, even though one might largely accept the merits of empowerment, the unquestioned adoption of such an approach, without considering factors that influence the sporting and athletes' world, places it in danger of becoming just another tool in a 'kit bag of quick fixes' (Whitmore, 1996, p. 27). It must be recognised that the coach is much more than someone who applies a particular method (Squires, 1999), given that it has become increasingly acknowledged that sports performance is not an exact science (Lyle, 1986).

The application of any coaching strategy, therefore, requires deliberation, reflection, imagination and flexibility. Indeed, coaching is fundamentally about making many differing connections, not only to and between subjects and methods, but also to and between other people and life in general (Armour & Fernandez-Balboa, 2000). It is a process that deserves and requires consideration of the particular situation and often imaginative solutions. Hence, to avoid unthinking and unquestioning reactions from 'cardboard coaches' by encouraging a 'one-fit-all model', we need to consider the how, where and when of implementing a philosophy such as empowerment.

To consider such implementation in depth, the coach must examine the unique social and environmental features of the local situation, before acting accordingly. In other words, if the end goal is to empower athletes, the coach should exercise care and sensitivity in working towards that goal with varying groups, taking account of the particular context or circumstance. For example, a coach trying to implement an empowerment philosophy with younger children will encounter different barriers from a coach who is dealing with elite athletes. No doubt the philosophy can and should be implemented with both groups, but the speed, method and means of implementation must vary with the circumstance if the strategy is to be successfully adopted.

Aim of this Chapter

In the previous chapters, some coaches have discussed how they have implemented an empowerment approach, along with some of the perceived benefits and challenges of their respective experiences. In the next chapter, 'voice' is given to two élite athletes who express their responses to an empowering approach. I use this chapter to elaborate on some of the issues highlighted by these coaches and athletes, and raise additional issues associated with implementing such a strategy.

The purpose of this chapter, therefore, is to illustrate how coaches can implement an empowerment model in a range of situations. It highlights some of the potential difficulties in adopting such an approach with differing athletic populations and how coaches can overcome such difficulties. It indicates some complex links between theory and practice, emphasising the need to understand local circumstances as they can impact on the implementation of a new strategy, such as empowerment. The intent is to assist coaches understand how, when and where empowerment can best be introduced to their athletes as a performance concept. In this respect, the coaching process is viewed as a holistic entity as opposed to the model often presented to prospective coaches, in which coaching comprises unconnected, 'ready-made' knowledge (Jones, in press). In this chapter, it is advocated that there is no prescriptive formula regarding how coaches can implement empowerment, as its use requires continued self-analysis (see Chapter Ten) to develop ideas appropriate to each coach's particular circumstances.

The chapter is broadly divided into two related sections. First, issues in applying an empowerment philosophy in children's sport are examined. Implementation in this area includes the challenge of convincing parents that an empowerment approach, which often appears unstructured to the unaware observer, has educational and sporting value. Second, some potential problems related to initiating an empowerment strategy with élite or senior athletes are investigated, together with some suggested solutions.

Implementing Empowerment in Children's Sport

Although on first examination, the introduction of an empowerment philosophy when coaching children would appear to be generally straightforward, the issue is less clear-cut on deeper analysis. The principal difficulty here arises from children's perception of the coach as holding an 'expert' role, and the coach's great power that derives simply from his or her perceived role, title and actual size(!) in comparison to the child-athlete. As a result, typically children appear to accept the dictates and requests of the coach, easily and totally. Thus they are likely to accept a new approach, be it an attempt at empowering athletes or otherwise, in a similarly unquestioning manner.

Unfortunately, if athletes accept an empowerment approach without question, they may well develop only a superficial understanding of the goals of empowerment, rather than the desired levels of self-evaluation and self-reliance. Ironically, a philosophy that emphasises independence of thought and self-responsibility, may be unquestioningly accepted by athletes, simply because a coach wishes to use it!

A further problem with implementing such a strategy with children is the risk of the questioning degenerating into a 'free-for-all' response session. As a result, time for worthwhile practice can be lost. Moreover, if the session is allowed to spiral out of control, it can divide the group both sportingly and socially.

To overcome such challenges, a coach must tread warily and considerately, initially making sure that the athletes understand the ultimate goals of the philosophy, and also that they are sincerely buying in to the new strategy. In this way, the coach ensures that the athletes realise how the new approach can help them reach their goals. To introduce empowerment, the coach should carefully and realistically explain its aims and methods before launching into a series of questions. The aim of such questions should be not only to identify the motivations and goals of the children, but also to check their understanding of the objective of the exercises and how both the approach and the drills benefit their sporting development. In turn the rate, depth and content of the questioning inevitably depends on the receptiveness of the children to the approach, which is reliant on their abilities, maturity and reasons for participating. In short, to have athletes buy in to empowerment, or any approach, a coach must ensure that athletes realise and accept its value, a process that often varies with the individual athlete.

Questioning children

What sort of questions, then, would a coach ask children (see also Chapter Eight)? Taking account of situational factors as mentioned above, the coach could initially focus on relatively simple task-specific issues. For example, in developing tennis ground strokes, the coach may ask the athlete which way the ball is spinning as it comes toward him or her over the net and how it is likely to move after it has bounced. Similar clues are found in answering and reflecting on questions surrounding the height and speed of the approaching ball, in addition to the follow through of the opponent. If the athlete 'reads' and understands these clues, it should ensure his or her best preparation for a return shot.

In this way, the child learns to execute the task better through self-evaluation and awareness of his or her actions. More than that, the child develops a greater understanding of the game itself. As Whitmore (1996, p. 43) noted, 'the coach needs to probe deeper for more detail to keep the coachee involved and to bring into his [sic] consciousness those often partially obscured factors that may be important'. Such a line of questioning also encourages children to take greater responsibility over their actions and respective performances, which also increases their commitment to the stated goal.

Once the athletes are happy with accepting this increased responsibility, the coach can expand the questioning to include other features of the performance, such as game plans. Constant, although not tedious, questioning of various performance aspects can both develop the mental aspects of an athlete's performance and increase commitment to the performance. Such questions could relate to why a task was performed in a specific way, the possible consequences, and the aims of different team formations and the best responses to them.

An important point to decide on here is which areas of athletes' performances to question. The ideal answer is to allow the athletes to identify the areas they wish to work on, thus further empowering them in their quest to improve. This approach also allows the athletes the opportunity to explore avenues of their respective performances in which they have an interest (Whitmore, 1996). However, it could prove counterproductive to leave this process to be entirely athlete-led, if the child chooses to avoid difficult tasks. Consequently, the coach has a role in exploring those avenues that the athlete does not bring forward, but that the coach perceives as needing attention. To ensure that the athlete drives the process however, the coach could introduce such issues by questioning why the athlete has not mentioned a certain aspect of performance so far (Whitmore, 1996). In this way, the coach leaves the athlete to take the initiative in addressing the point at hand.

Questioning adolescents

When working with adolescents in this questioning way, the coach needs to consider further issues, as these athletes often are more anxious with regard to their own identity. Their anxiety increases when they are subject to public display and perceived evaluation, such as in a training session or sporting event, especially in front of their peers (Roberts & Treasure, 1993). Research has shown how important the general sport experience is for this age group, particularly in terms of their peer relationships and perceived self-worth (Roberts, 1984).

Therefore, if the coach uses an overly aggressive questioning style such that an athlete feels deficient, obviously the result could be counterproductive. Adolescents who fail to demonstrate knowledge and ability in sport, as an activity that is particularly valued, are likely to find the experience 'extremely stressful' (Roberts & Treasure, 1993, p. 6). Thus the coach should take care to avoid drawing attention to any perceived inadequacy that could result if an athlete is unable to answer the questions asked.

Conversely, some adolescents may see a questioning strategy as an opportunity to demonstrate their knowledge and to 'be better than others' in an aspect of sport, thus fostering a competitive 'win at all costs' sporting climate. Such an environment runs contrary to an empowering approach, which highlights performance rather than outcome and is related to satisfaction in sport, to learning and to the belief that sport enhances social responsibility (Roberts & Treasure, 1993). Such a philosophy is also associated with an ability to evaluate one's own performances and adapt accordingly (Roberts & Treasure, 1993). Consequently, a coach must take additional care of specific individual needs and issues when working with adolescents to ensure that they gain an empowering experience.

Parental attitudes and the coach's credibility

It has been repeatedly established that for children to derive a positive learning experience from sports participation, parents need to be aware of their own role and influence in the process (Kidman, 1998). Research has also provided valuable evidence that parents not only have a major influence over why children participate in sport, but also are socialising agents in helping shape the values that children derive from sport. Consequently, parents need to act with the intention of promoting successful performance experiences for their children in sport rather than focusing on outcomes and results (Roberts & Treasure, 1993). In this way, they should be aware of the need to reduce the level of open social evaluation (such as comments from the sideline), encourage children's notion of success (i.e. to have fun, meet new friends and improve skills) and enhance children's self-esteem through appropriate supportive behaviours. An empowerment approach supports these goals as it focuses on the sporting process and the success of athletes.

Many parents, however, have a very specific view of how coaches should coach. Their own past experiences as athletes, combined with a natural desire for the best for their children, mean that coaches often face a real challenge in convincing such parents about the value of an 'alternative' approach such as empowerment. Again, there are no 'quick-fix' solutions, but the following ideas about how to educate parents provide some meaningful food for thought.

Hugh Galvan (in Chapter Four) suggests that open communication is a key to educating parents about coaching philosophies. As part of their current rugby season, Hugh and Paul McKay held a meeting with their players at the first training session where the reasons that individual players were involved in rugby were discussed and the team's direction for the season was mutually agreed. Being aware of the potential difficulties in convincing parents of this 'alternative' empowerment approach and having experienced 'pushy parent' syndrome previously, Hugh then decided to try open communication with the parents in an attempt to circumvent related problems. The approach he tried was:

> ... to send a newsletter home to the parents outlining what our beliefs and philosophies were to keep them informed ... We brought them together on the very first day for a meeting and reinforced what we were trying to achieve. We told them that it probably wasn't what they were used to, but that it was what the players had suggested, so it was going to be of benefit to them.

Hugh and Paul were very pleased by the parental response to the initiative. Parents adjusted their expectations when they learned about the philosophy and direction the team had chosen to adopt at the beginning of the season. They were also able to see and appreciate the benefits of such an approach as the season progressed. These parents seem to have been convinced.

Holding a meeting at the beginning of a season has been acknowledged as an appropriate way to communicate philosophies and expectations to parents (Kidman & McKenzie, 1999). Such a meeting should include a discussion of the team's shared philosophy along with the various expectations expressed by athletes and coaches. The parents, in turn, should have an opportunity to ask questions and provide input and comment within the meeting's structure. Through such involvement, parents are encouraged to feel a degree of ownership over the team's direction and goals, and thus are much more prepared to buy in to the overriding philosophy and accompanying methods of the coach.

Throughout the season, as part of their open communication policy, Hugh and Paul reinforced parents' positive comments on the sidelines. They also continued to remind players and parents of the goals and directions that they had mutually decided for the season. They believed this approach to communication was a key to dealing with the potentially problematic circumstances that arose from time to time. Additionally, Hugh and Paul believed that their strategy enabled the parents to become aware of their own attitudes and values through observing how players gained enjoyment and success from participating in an 'empowering' team.

It is difficult to gauge truly how parents are responding to an empowering approach, as little research has been carried out on the issue to date. What is known, however, is that some parents place so much pressure on their children to 'win' in sport that it can actually decrease the children's enjoyment of the activity, to the extent that they may wish to drop out altogether. On the other hand, if the children buy in to an empowerment approach, it often appears that they can convince their parents of its benefits too. In this way, parents can indirectly come to accept such a philosophy. However, coaches can aid this process greatly by establishing and maintaining an open communication policy with parents, and thereafter dealing with any problems that may arise with honesty and integrity.

Wayne Smith has suggested that to convince the public (including parents) of an empowerment approach, a coach must first gain personal and philosophical credibility. In this respect, each coach is responsible for gaining credibility through his or her actions, which will, in turn, convince parents of the value of the approach. If coaches can demonstrate a team environment where children are having fun, are successful, are clearly learning and wish to continue to participate after the season ends, they will easily obtain that credibility.

Implementing Empowerment with Élite Athletes

Although perhaps pouring a dash of cold realism on thoughts of adopting an empowerment coaching philosophy, it is recognised that it would be somewhat unrealistic to expect senior athletes and players, in particular, to embrace it willingly (see Chapters Three, Four and Six). Indeed, why should they, when perhaps they have achieved considerable success with coaches who have adopted prescriptive coaching to varying degrees? In such instances, it would be natural for athletes to resist a new coaching style, as often they have been socialised into expecting, and consequently desiring, considerable levels of instruction.

Many athletes prefer coaching that contains a high quota of prescriptive actions, regardless of the view (as advanced in this book) that such behaviour is disempowering, as it allows the athletes to avoid extensive mental consideration and responsibility. It is often much easier to react unquestioningly to a command than to reflect on how and why one performed a particular action or task. Similarly, when first learning an empowerment approach, many athletes are unable to deal with the idea that there are many 'right' ways to do things depending on the individual and his or her capabilities. Instead, they assume there is only one correct way, the way they have always done it (Rink et al., 1996). Consequently, there is no questioning as to why things are done in a certain way, just an acceptance that they are. It is a comfort zone that some athletes are reluctant to leave. How then should a coach react when faced with such resistance?

Starting on the right foot

The first step is to appropriately evaluate the athlete population that one is coaching. Before a coach can begin to apply an empowerment strategy, he or she should informally ask the athletes about their goals, motives and expectations. Their answers should indicate how these athletes would react to a new philosophy, particularly one that questions their past actions and asks them for a much higher degree of mental investment in their performances. It would be naïve to expect all athletes to immediately and enthusiastically accept a philosophy that aims to give them ownership of the team direction. Therefore the coach must identify an appropriate starting point for implementing empowerment and plan how to proceed from it.

Coaches need to introduce empowerment carefully and sensitively, gradually divesting their prescriptive power as and when they judge their athletes are ready to receive it. It would be beneficial for coaches to reflect on the nature and extent of the initial questions for the athletes, as the empowerment philosophy stems fundamentally from such actions. For example, if the athletes appear willing to adopt the philosophy from the outset, the empowerment could well begin with an examination of their self-defined needs and hopes, both individually and as a group (Arai, 1997). An exploration of differing and deeper aspects of their performances and goals could then soon, and easily, follow.

However, if some initial resistance to the strategy is evident, then the coach could adopt a more gradual approach to implementation. For example, as Paul McKay points out in Chapter Four, perhaps a coach could still engage in a certain degree of prescription, by putting a game plan and team framework in place, or even outlining the roles and responsibilities of individual players within team sports to some extent. In this way, the coach maintains part of the comfort zone for the athletes, as they perceive a continuation of the coach-imposed structure that has assisted them so far in their quest for success. If a coach leaves such a definite framework in place without player input, however, the athletes could come to view themselves as instruments merely functioning to fulfil organisational goals (Pratt & Eitzen, 1989), rather than their own.

Thus where the coach chooses to retain prescriptive elements, it is important to treat this situation as only a starting base from which to evolve a philosophy of common aims and shared ownership. As discussed above with regard to children, the coach could then begin to introduce empowerment through questioning the actions of players within the structure, focusing on why they acted in particular ways and what the consequences are for other team members. Through reflecting on their performances in this way, players are much more likely to take ownership of and responsibility for what they do. They also become increasingly aware of different options, thus giving them greater control over future directions (Arai, 1997; Freysinger & Bedini, 1994).

As well as developing a greater understanding of the game by reflecting on purposeful questions, athletes will also learn tactical skills more efficiently and effectively when they see the need for the skill to be developed (Rink et al., 1996). An empowerment approach gives them this opportunity as it focuses on issues of relevance and performance effectiveness (Freysinger & Bedini, 1994). Although success on the sports field might not be immediate, the first goal of empowerment, as when coaching children, is to get athletes to buy in to the philosophy. Therefore the coach needs to invest some time initially in developing athletes' understanding of the game or their sport, and of how their actions on the playing field have consequences for the following play and the wider team performance. As Usher (1997) noted, empowerment is a process whereby coaches produce results by providing the necessary environment in which athletes can develop their skills and understanding.

Cultivating a mutual environment

As briefly discussed in Chapter One, the coach needs to create an environment focused on mutuality, so that individuals and teams can grow in the same direction with a shared vision of goals and the means to get there. The real issues for coaches to address are the pace and methods of establishing and cultivating such an environment.

In this respect, through the coach's gradual development of questioning, athletes first learn the aims of the new strategy and later, through the coach's measured implementation, take ownership over their learning and knowledge. As athletes and players begin to see the benefits of the strategy, they come to increasingly believe in it, thus they become willing to take more responsibility for what they do and learn. Consequently, rather than questioning the athletes only on their actions within games and resultant general performances, the coach can expand the empowerment of athletes by seeking their input on season goals, appropriate fitness levels and team strategies.

Specifically, this greater empowerment could involve the athletes having a say in team formations, tactics and set plays. Perhaps it would be unrealistic to expect athletes to take total control over such issues, as it must be expected, and to an extent respected, that there will be dissenting voices within teams, reflecting individual personalities. Therefore the coach still has an active role in ensuring that the team talks out any disagreements constructively within a given framework.

A coach's role in the process thus evolves from an instructor to a facilitator who guides the athletes to their preferred solution. It could be argued that with the coach remaining at the helm, albeit in an altered role, the athletes experience only an illusion of empowerment, rather than true empowerment itself. However, such a stance ignores how athletes' perception that they are contributing builds their self-esteem, and how the process of reflecting on knowledge, and decision-making and its consequences, has obvious value in personal development. Consequently, within a philosophy of empowerment, coaches can be viewed as 'agents of learning who help athletes understand how to exceed their current limits; it is a role of nurturing involvement and autonomy in the learning athlete' (Usher, 1997, p. 11).

Conclusion

Perhaps the hardest part of implementing a theory of empowerment at any level is having the patience to let it run at the speed of the athletes (Arai, 1997). This pace, as Arai (1997) notes, is often much slower than a coach imagines. The athletes must first become open to change, which expresses itself in a need and desire for it, and a recognition of its value. Remaining patient is not always easy for coaches, who traditionally like, and often need, short-term gratification and results from their work. If coaches try to force this change, however, they are likely to hinder athletes' acceptance of the philosophy and instead create resistance to its adoption. Therefore a prerequisite of successful implementation is to patiently support and encourage the athletes to accept and integrate the empowerment philosophy at their own speed. To achieve a shared ownership of common goals, a coach must respect the individuality of each athlete.

It is important to remember that empowerment is never truly complete, as new challenges continually rise; these challenges are often linked to the uniqueness of each athlete, the interaction between athletes and the particular context of each interaction. As Arai (1997) notes, 'it is a long journey of dialogue and supporting individual development' (p. 10), which, to be successfully implemented and adopted, must take the environment and circumstances into account. In this respect, the process of empowerment is complex, as it 'forces us to reflect on the interaction among a myriad of forces at play within an individual's life' (Arai, 1997, p. 10). As all coaches know, such reflection is not an easy task but it is certainly worthwhile if the process results in mature, independent and creatively thinking athletes.

References

Arai, S.M. (1997). Empowerment: from the theoretical to the personal, *Journal of Leisurability, 24*(1), 3–11.

Armour, K.M., & Fernandez-Balboa, J.M. (2000). Connections, pedagogy and professional learning. Paper presented at CEDAR 8th International Conference, University of Warwick, England, 20–22 March.

Butler, J. (1997). How would Socrates teach games? A constructivist approach, *Journal of Physical Education, Recreation and Dance, 68*(9), 42–47.

Freysinger, V., & Bedini, L.A. (1994). Teaching for empowerment, *Journal of Leisure Studies and Recreational Education, 9,* 1–11.

Jones, R.L. (in press). Toward a sociology of coaching. In R.L. Jones & K.M. Armour (eds), *The Sociology of Sport in Practice.* London: Addison-Wesley-Longman.

Jones, R.L. & Armour, K. (under review). The cultures of coaching.

Kidman, L. (1998). Who reaps the benefits in coaching research? The case for an applied sociological approach, *Sociology of Sport On Line, 1*(2), 1 <www.brunel.ac.uk/depts/sps/sosol/v1i2.htm>

Kidman, L., & McKenzie, A. (1999). *Join the Team: A Guide for Parents/Caregivers in Sport.* Australian Sport Commission.

Lyle, J. (1986). Coach education: preparation for a profession. *In Proceedings of the VIII Commonwealth and International Conference on Sport, Physical Education, Dance, Recreation and Health* (pp. 1–25). London: F.N. Spon.

Pratt, S.R., & Eitzen, D.S. (1989). Contrasting leadership styles and organisational effectiveness: the case of athletic teams, *Social Science Quarterly, 70*(2), 311–322.

Rink, J.E., French, K.E., & Tjeerdsma, B.L. (1996). Foundations for the learning of instruction of sport and games, *Journal of Teaching in Physical Education, 15,* 399–417.

Roberts, G. (1984). Achievement motivation in children's sport. In J. Nicholls (ed.), *The Development of Achievement Motivation* (pp. 251–281). Greenwich, CT: JAI Press.

Roberts, G., & Treasure, D. (1993). The importance of the study of children in sport: an overview. In M. Lee (ed.), *Coaching Children in Sport: Principles and Practice* (pp. 3–16). London: E. & F.N. Spon.

Squires, G. (1999). *Teaching as a Professional Discipline.* London: Falmer Press.

Usher, R. (1997). Empowerment as a powerful coaching tool, *Coaches' Report, 4*(2), 10–11.

Usher, R. (1998). The story of the self: education, experience and autobiography. In M. Erben (ed.), *Biography and Education: A Reader* (pp. 18–31). London: Falmer Press.

Whitmore, J. (1996) (2nd ed.). *Coaching for Performance.* London: Nicholas Brealey.

Coaches have to watch for what they don't want to see and listen to what they don't want to hear.

—John Madden

Fathers and mothers have lost the idea that the highest aspiration they might have for their children is for them to be wise ... specialized competence and success are all that they can imagine.

—Allan Bloom

Chapter Six

A wise man makes his own decisions, an ignorant man follows the public opinion.

—Chinese Proverb

What do Athletes Say about an Empowerment Approach? Perspectives from Anna Veronese and Daryl Gibson

To gain a fuller understanding of how athletes perceive this empowering approach, interviews were conducted with two 'élite' athletes. The athletes have trained under coaches who took a prescriptive approach, as well as coaches who followed an empowerment approach—particularly Wayne Smith (national and regional rugby coach: see Chapter Three) for Daryl Gibson, and Leigh Gibbs (national and regional netball coach) for Anna Veronese. It is clear from the interviews that both athletes preferred coaching that involved an empowerment approach, but for very different reasons. Both highlight the benefits of empowerment to enhance the team culture and the difference a good team culture makes to their performance.

Daryl Gibson played for the Canterbury Crusaders rugby team for the three years that Wayne Smith was the team's coach. He has been an All Black and captained the Canterbury team in the National Provincial Championships (NPC) 2000. Daryl has followed through with career ambitions (outside of rugby) to enhance his personal and professional life. Both Wayne Smith and Daryl believe that players should be encouraged to be more than just rugby jocks. They also believe that having outside interests enhances players' ability to perform. After training as a teacher of physical education, Daryl completed a Masters of Education in 2000.

Anna Veronese has played for the Canterbury Flames (a regional women's netball team) for four years as well as for the Canterbury NPC team for several years. In 2000 Anna played for the New Zealand netball team, the Silver Ferns. Anna, like Daryl, has pursued qualifications for a career while competing in netball. She firmly believes that a balanced lifestyle is the key to success in sport and in life. Anna completed a Bachelor of Education with a specialisation in physical education in 2000 and is now a trained physical education teacher.

What is Empowerment?

First the athletes were asked to explain what they think an empowerment coaching approach is:

Daryl: I think it is a way that coaches use to give players ownership or control over their actions in training. It's also a way, in terms of Wayne, I see him using it, he always observes and stops, like the way the teachers use the style. He generates a lot of questions about situations or drills and asks players how they can improve. He is always asking for their feedback and solutions to a problem. So he never actually gives the right answer, or there may not be a right answer, but he is always generating the answer from the player.

[An example is if the player's performance] is falling down or some problem or something wrong with the move or some body language or something, he will question that player and say, 'What if you did this? What if you did that better? What can you improve?' They are always coming up with the answers.

Anna: Empowering, to me, involves getting the athletes to come up with the answers and feel like they have ownership of what they are trying to achieve or what it is you are trying to teach them. Therefore, when placed in a challenging situation in the game, they [the athletes] can work through the answers and think for themselves.

I have had coaches in the past and I still have coaches who tell us every movement that we need to make. They may say something like, 'We are playing Team A, and this is the style they play and this what we are going to do'. The game plan is almost like a lecture. To me, empowerment is giving the athletes credit for having intelligence to be able to think for themselves. After all it is the athletes that are making the decisions in pressure situations in the game. That's exactly how I see it, athletes can think for themselves, we do the research, we are intelligent people, we can sit down … with our teammates and work it out. Obviously, we need help from our coaches and whoever else assists us. We are always learning.

Both athletes were asked if they preferred the empowerment approach

over other approaches:

Daryl: I like it, I definitely like it mainly because I come from a teaching background and it suits what I have been influenced by. It also gives the player an opportunity to have input into the team and what they are doing. Yes, for me it is a good method.

Anna: Personally, I like it when Leigh says, 'Why did you do that?' because then you get to work through the reasons why you moved somewhere, or what you did wrong, which brings you to a higher level of understanding ... to try and work it out.

You also get a chance to say why you thought you should move to that position. It might not necessarily be the right place to go, but at least you can work through it.

I find I need to have the reasoning and knowledge of why I need to change rather than just being told that it was not right. If this is given, yes I think the next time (or possibly after a couple of times of Leigh saying, 'Ah, you just did it again' or 'What did you do then?') I would be able to adapt and change. I need to understand why. I don't just go somewhere when I am marking my opponent. It is all fairly structured on defence.

Sometimes I get really frustrated. Especially if I remember back to when I was playing in the goal keep position, which is a very tactical and specific position. If I got on the wrong side of my opponent, and the ball went straight into the circle, then you feel annoyed, and you look silly because the ball has just gone straight into the goal circle. If the coach also yells at you, it can get demoralising because you know you've made a mistake, as does everyone else. This may result in thinking negative thoughts about your play, which will naturally be detrimental to your performance.

Do Daryl and Anna think that most athletes accept an empowerment approach? Is there any resistance to it among their teammates?

Daryl: I think the Crusaders, and Wayne in particular, had quite progressive drills. We like to be innovative and we see the game development and have a progression of drills to suit that. I think a lot of teams in other franchises were slow to accept that, that this is the way the game is going and these are the drills that will facilitate that.

In terms of that, I can remember a lot of players saying, 'Oh why are we doing this and why exactly should we be doing this'? There was a lot of resistance to actual change. I think that would be one of the biggest. I think being outside and looking at the All Blacks this year, I can see them because there are a large group from Canterbury, that sort of resistance or reluctance to change the old ways has dissipated. The fact that there are a lot less players who are reluctant to change their ways and be progressive has helped in that transformation.

Anna: [I asked one of the players and] she said, 'I hate when Leigh stopped training if I had done something wrong'. For example, Leigh might ask, 'Why did you pass the ball there?' and she said that she hadn't thought about it and she didn't like it when Leigh asked her to stop and think about it. She said she was a doer rather than a thinker and that she just wanted to get out there. I think it was because she doesn't like being put on the spot and maybe also because the coach did not explain their methodology at the beginning of the season. I think she might have felt picked on.

I know there will be some people who don't know what empowerment is, have never heard of it, or have never been exposed to the different philosophies of coaching or team culture. If they've never been exposed to it, they would have no idea what was going on. As a coach it is important to explain at the beginning of the season what it is that you are trying to do, especially if you do intend on trying something that people may not have been exposed to before.

So do the athletes who resisted the empowerment approach, now appreciate it?

Daryl: I think so. I can remember reading that article about Craig Dowd in the paper saying that he loves it and that he has totally bought into it. He's a player who has seen a lot of different coaching styles and methods and has been successful with them, I would imagine he has to adapt to a new regime and method.

That is the difficult part. Last four weeks or five weeks, we've had a completely new team. Getting a team of new players to that same level and teaching them all the drills, that [is] quite tiresome, but you have to go through that to get … everyone up to the same level.

Anna: No … [because] it wasn't explained.

The athletes were asked if their coaches with an empowerment approach ever revert back to their old 'prescriptive' style of coaching:

Daryl: Yes, … particularly to the forwards, when they are unsure of what exactly they are supposed to be doing when they are in the back line, for example. He would direct them, like 'This is where you are standing, this is the line you run.'

… in terms of a coach motivating a team, I think he [Wayne] tries to be more authoritative in his giving of instructions. To me, he is not, sort of. Well, you have coaches that are more 'rah, rah, rah', not really technical, but man-management type of people. I think that is one area he has tried to develop within himself. Because you have always known him as a facilitator and empowerer, you never see him as a 'rah, rah, rah' sort of guy. I have seen it occasionally, but everyone was sort of taken aback by it, wondering what was wrong with Smithy. We would tell him, 'Look mate, you'd better calm down, making us all edgy.'

Anna: Leigh has always been an empowering-type coach, she has never been into telling us what to do, but tries to get the information out of us. I'm sure Leigh is refining this methodology more each year and I am looking forward to the 2001 season.

Anna also speaks about another coach who is trialling the empowerment approach:

Anna: I think she is learning to become an empowering-type coach as well. I have definitely found Marg [Foster], especially towards the end of this season, to be an empowering coach. She began to ask us things like, 'Why did you go there?' if you drove the wrong way on an attack play through court. Marg is definitely a coach who strives to get the best out of each of her players. She knows that everyone is an individual and therefore he or she may need to be handled differently from some of the other members of the team.

Marg was never a directive-style coach, but ... she has definitely moved along the continuum more towards empowerment. One day, I did something and I can remember her saying, 'Why was that not a good pass to make?' She tried to let me work through and understand why I made that decision. I was able to work through the poor passing option that I made and came to realise that I had landed off-balance, which had affected my vision, and therefore I did not deliver the ball to the best passing option.

Anna suggests that sometimes coaches fall back into the prescriptive style when there is time pressure, because of the time involved in asking questions:

Anna: In the heat of the moment, the coach is likely to jump in and tell you. This is due to the time factor. If the coach wants us to work [with] intensity for 15 minutes, they are not going to want to stop for two minutes and find out why I stepped when I caught the ball, if they know that I know the answer or it was just a simple mistake. I'm sure they would just tell me in this situation.

Being Questioned

In Chapter Five, Robyn Jones suggests that one of the major concerns for athletes to overcome is how to respond to questions when they are unaccustomed to being asked for their input. Both Daryl and Anna note that many of the players hesitate to answer questions:

Daryl: I think there are a few people taken [a]back by it and those who are shy ..., perhaps that is what they were like at school and they feel like they [are] back at school with this type of questioning?

If they are new to it, they think, 'Don't ask me because I don't really know the answer', or 'There are a range of answers and I not sure which one the coach wants to hear'. If the coach is good at questioning, then they should be able to elicit the right response. Eventually, you will get to the right answer or an answer to what you want, but the player is getting to have input.

'How can we attack where the space [is], where the two players are?', he probably would ask. So, it's really an education process that we embark on through doing that. Straight away you know that you are looking for space. He demonstrates the actual way to do it plus options. Especially if he is teaching you something, like it could be something about passing. He demonstrates it first, then he tries to generate why, why you do that. He is more directed [in his] approach. I can't ever remember him saying, 'This is the objective of a drill'. I am sure he would teach first, work, teach, work, teach, work and question.

Anna: Often, when Leigh asks us questions, it is the same four or five people answering. The others may feel like their input is not worthwhile or they may simply not know the answer. There are definitely people in our team that feel a little threatened when faced with a question. If a coach is good at questioning, he/she should be able to ensure that these team members have input as well.

The two athletes were asked about the coach's ability to question:

Daryl: It's probably more relying on the coach to have the skills to facilitate the question to have good questioning skills basically … and the way you construct, whether it is an open question or a closed question.

Anna: Often, I see the teacher in Leigh coming out. She asks us questions then adds her bit, so really sometime the answer[s] end up being her own. Teachers are often very directive, I don't think a teacher necessarily makes a good coach. It's the questioning and listening skills that are necessary as a coach.

Teaching Game Sense

The athletes were asked about their understanding of Game Sense, or Games for Understanding (see Chapter Two):

Daryl: Most of the drills are all constructed in that sort of manner [game-like situations]. They are designed on the basic principles of rugby—go forward and using space. Probably the greatest thing I've noticed over the three years when Wayne first started [with] the team is the education of the player. The fact that everyone knows the principles of rugby quite clearly, regardless of whether you are a prop or fullback, everyone knows exactly what we are trying to achieve. I think that has been one of the greatest improvements, the fact that the game has changed to a degree where everyone has to do everyone's role. The modern rugby player must be multi-skilled and able to perform all the necessary skills well. To be able to do this you must know the facets of each position, their responsibilities.

… but we play a lot of games. He got much of this [range of games] from the Brisbane Broncos. [For example,] you have two tackle bags, two hit shields and there is a line, one is attacking with the ball. This guy as a defensive player, goes back and calls two numbers, they drop out and go.

Anna: I totally agree with Game Sense and the fact that the more specific to the game that your training is, the more beneficial it will be. With the Silver Ferns, Robyn [Broughton] would give us a scenario like, 'Two minutes to go and you are down by three points'. Every single person then begins to work very hard, playing like it is a game. The attackers are going hard out to get those three goals and the defence are thinking, 'We are ahead by three, and we are not going to let the attackers beat us'. By training with your teammates in this type of situation, you are bringing the standard of the whole team up by pushing each other's limits.

There are a lot of skills you use in netball that are usually limited to a tight game where it is goal for goal. If we can train ourselves to use these 'street skills' at training then we will be better in a game situation.

Game Sense increases our motivation too … we all like playing the game, don't we? [In Game Sense] you expend more effort. The game is the pinnacle event, therefore the more game-like training sessions in which I am participating, the more motivated I become and therefore harder I train.

Athlete Input

Both athletes suggest that it is important for athletes to have a say in determining the vision and goals for the team at the beginning of the season. Daryl elaborates on how the Crusaders determine their vision and goals:

Daryl: … somehow they present it [vision and goals] to you in some form. We had a card that was like a credit card. I can't remember what they [vision and goals] were. I remember the NPC ones … enjoyment, sacrifices, fronting. All these words encompass different meanings, like honesty associated with fronting. It triggers you to think basically. You get discipline and all this.

Anna was asked how her teams have decided on their visions and goals for the season and which decision-making method she preferred:

Anna: I don't know what [our coach] is going to do this season yet, but I would say she is going to move towards sitting us down as a whole team and making team goals pre-season. Margaret Foster did that with the Flames last year. She sat us down as a complete unit at the beginning of the year. Together we worked out what we wanted to do, where we were heading and what we wanted to achieve in the year.

At the beginning of the season, [Marg] got everyone in together, the whole team unit, the coach, the assistant coach, the physio, the manager and all the players. Together we decided what it is that we wanted to achieve for the season. When you have ownership of the goals not only as a player but as a whole team unit, I find everyone is like, 'Right, we have set this down for us to achieve, we are the ones who have come up with it, we're the ones that need to action it and make it happen'. The coach can't really make that happen in isolation. It is hard to follow or act out someone else's vision, but when the goals/visions are your own, you take ownership and work together to achieve them.

So how does Marg follow through with establishing a team vision or several visions?

Anna: We came up with a sheet of 10 visions. Marg printed them out and we had a Canterbury Flames booklet and it was there for all to see and she referred to it quite often during the season. There were things like, 'Don't bring your baggage to training'.

Marg did different things with us in 2000 that we had not been exposed to previously. For example, at the beginning of each training you had to rate how you were feeling out of 10—10 being the best—and then give one word to describe how you were feeling. You might say, 'Three, sick' or 'Eight, excited'. Marg would adapt training based on team member's ratings and feelings. If most people were low, she'd say, 'Right, no one here is ready to do an intense training session, so I am going lower the intensity a bit. We'll go for quality not quantity.' She was flexible; she would listen to us, which we really appreciated.

... everyone felt like they were important and it enabled us to let our team members know how you were feeling. If someone had given a rating of three and said they were stressed out, you would know that during that particular training session you just had to lay off that person a bit. It was not a case of being 'soft' on one another, it was just knowing where people were at on a day-to-day basis.

In Chapter Three, Wayne discusses the value of having Gilbert Enoka to help with developing team goals and visions. Daryl was asked about Gilbert Enoka and his role with the Crusaders:

Daryl: He doesn't really do a lot with the Crusaders this year, but more in the past, he does a lot behind the scene ... It's a voluntary [decision] to go see Gilbert. You don't have to see him. You don't have to see him in the review system. He got books and review books that you can do on each game, etc., but if you don't want to use it, you don't have to. As long as you are doing something. [I don't do much with him,] not goals. I do it in my head, but not on a piece of paper like they would like you to do.

... one of the biggest things [is], we don't ever set goals to win. We say that we can't be outcome-orientated, we are performance-orientated. So, week to week, ... we do what is in the present.

Daryl was asked if he is allowed to give feedback to his coaches about coaching:

Daryl: Yes, they do that but usually it comes from the player, who says, 'Why don't we do this?' And they say, 'Okay, that's cool.' So the player is always offering their advice and the coach saying that they think it looks cool, or it would be better if we did this.

[Wayne's] first year particularly, he was really stressed, frustrated and stressed with players and he was probably taking it out on us. He was probably yelling, which was very uncommon for him. A few players mentioned to him, 'Look we really don't respond well to that.' … He took it on board.

This year on the Crusaders, we had a drills committee which was me and my job was to basically come up with new drills, and I'm always offering them to coaches and they say yes or no.

Even though coaches ask for feedback, Daryl alludes, ultimately they still hold the power in the team because, for example, they are the selectors:

Daryl: It is professional. They pick the team. If you are not picked you don't get paid. Like Aaron Flynn, he got knocked out, so he loses all of his NPC pay. So straight away, he has to go and find another team or he doesn't get paid. It is probably more important for the Super 12 as if you don't get selected for a Super 12 team, you are gone even if you have a three-year contract. It is year-to-year basically … it is much better to go overseas for security.

So would Daryl still play rugby if he didn't get paid? He says, 'you would still be doing it, but you wouldn't be committing as much time to it.'

Team Culture

Both Daryl and Anna comment on how their team culture was created:

Daryl: What happens at the start of the season is that the team sits down and plans the year. At planning we establish our culture which is the values that we share and believe in and that is a team process. We develop a whole list, we brainstorm the things that we value, and we put them up on a board. We then rationalise them, cut them down and see if we can … For each year it is different, there are things we want to focus on. We select the ones that [we] look upon as valuable …

The values are always in your mind and being reinforced. Yes, definitely. You have to work at it constantly. It's something that has always given us a little edge over other teams. I am sure if other teams start to do it … That is a huge part of it that people on the team are genuinely fun to be around and because they have all bought into it.

Anna: In Canterbury we have a really good team culture that has obviously been built up by the coach/coaches over the years and is still continuing to be built up. I think once the players start … developing a culture amongst themselves, the coaches can come and go, but the players will still have that link. So the coach can add to it and enhance it. I have had a coach that has done that.

I think when you have a directive-style coach, if people disagree or don't like what is going on, rather than talking about it amongst the team, it gets talked about among the players and that creates disharmony, which affects the team culture.

But when you have a coach who uses empowerment, where people are open and feel like they can talk about things and you know what the coach's philosophy is and where you are heading, it does make for a better team culture.

I have had a coach that has got along well with all the girls socially and that made a big difference. It was great when the coach joined in as well because she was involved in the team bonding out of training and off the court. A lot of coaches aren't really into that.

Wayne comments in Chapter Three that the Crusaders changed from an unconfident team to a very confident team. Does Daryl agree?

Daryl: Yes, there was starting to be a real belief in the team. The change took time … the Crusaders had finished last in the first season of the Super 12. We were really at rock bottom. Then he came along and I think started to educate the players on getting the basic skills right. He introduced his philosophies. They were pretty generic philosophies, focused on team culture. It was always there, it … just wasn't highlighted. He really made us focus on a good team culture.

To answer that question [about confidence], I quite enjoyed it. There was obviously some adjustments. I had just finished teacher's college and I was full of ideas. Because it was new, it took a while to adapt and change and also he had to change his approach in the way he handled stressful situations. That's the biggest thing that sticks in my mind for that year, … a few practices where he almost lost it because we weren't quite doing exactly … Following that, the next two years, he really changed.

In 1998, we embarked on creating themes and really getting back to values … and we used those values that we lived by. They came from us, the players … the players have to own them and live them. Great, we had just been through it with NPC last week and the players really live by them. Also we do a few things on the team to reinforce those values, like if you meet somebody, you have a special shake, hand shake.

Daryl was asked how the Crusaders team culture differed from the All Blacks team culture in 1999:

Daryl: Obviously the familiarity with each other. We didn't know each other in the All Blacks and the fact that the Crusaders had been together for three or four years. The majority of the [All Black] team, you didn't know too well. That was a major factor.

... I think a lot of the stuff from the team culture comes from the type of coaching style that is operated at the time. With the All Blacks, it was autocratic and very controlling. The players never really had a chance to contribute to the actual decision making. There were hints of empowerment, mainly because of Wayne's involvement, but ...

As in the Crusaders, the vision for the All Blacks was mutually established. However, Daryl indicates that the All Black vision and values 'were occasionally reinforced, but there wasn't that total buy-in to it and the fact that you are living your values day-to-day.'

In the year of the interview (2000), Daryl was picked as captain for the NPC Canterbury team. Is he an empowering or prescriptive captain?

Daryl: A bit of both actually. [In the game you have to be prescriptive] but in other decisions you ask other people's opinions. At training I would ask opinions to make sure they are comfortable with things.

Some Concluding Thoughts: Benefits and Challenges

Empowerment as an approach for children is very useful, according to Daryl:

Daryl: I think it would work better with children. I find myself, when I am doing coaching sessions, that I use it all the time to generate responses from them. Because obviously if they can do that, it can be self-served, they can learn why. I do a demonstration, but straight away, while I am doing a demonstration, to ask, to get responses from them, like what if I did this, what if I did that ...

... what Canterbury has tried to do is that they have a strong development programme and I am pretty sure that they are trying to mirror what is happening at the Crusaders, down to the colts and academy sides, so as soon one of the players get to the top they are ready.

Daryl also feels that the empowerment approach should be encouraged among more junior coaches:

Daryl: Yes, they should be getting those coaches from those teams, watching our trainings so they can take some of those drills back to their teams so it is a cycle.

Anna was asked if there was anything she wanted to add about the empowerment approach:

Anna: I really like the empowerment theory, mainly because I like to be treated as an intellectual athlete. Through years of playing and the people who influence you (players around you, coaches, friends, family) you do manage to learn a lot of things. It's nice to be asked, so you can start formulating your own ideas as well, if you don't know the answer it is a chance to learn from your coach/coaches and the players around you.

Overall, it makes you a better thinker, which makes you, in my opinion, a better player. Also in the big scheme of life, it makes you a better coach, a better teacher, a better parent or whatever it is you strive to be.

Daryl raises a few challenges for coaches and athletes when using the empowerment approach:

Daryl: I think the problem with the empowerment style is that occasionally you need to be autocratic and that there needs to be someone that is creating a direction. Certainly, I'd hate to have a coach who's autocratic and players don't have input. I believe … that all players have something to contribute to the team.

There weren't always the systems in place to do that, but now they are definitely. In the past, most coaches that I came across were pretty autocratic, they set the direction, they set everything.

It is interesting to note that, although these two athletes have been formally and substantially trained by prescriptive coaches and teachers, they feel all their coaches should use an empowerment approach. They point out that the approach is highly motivating, that athletes should take ownership of their sporting worlds and that they are very capable of making sound decisions. They both value the opportunity to make input to their own team and see the positive contribution a good team culture can make to the team and individual performance.

If coaches use an empowerment approach, athletes become better thinkers and thus better players. Great players are thinking players: as their comments show, both Anna and Daryl agree with this statement wholeheartedly.

Freedom is the opportunity to make decisions …

—*Kenneth Hildrebrand*

Talent wins games, but teamwork and intelligence win championships.

—*Michael Jordan*

Chapter Seven

Everybody wants to be somebody. The thing you have to do is give them confidence they can. You have to give a kid a dream.

—*George Foreman*

Have You Seen My Childhood? Understanding the Identity of the Athlete

Craig Lewis, Director of Sportlife New Zealand

Identifying yourself as an athlete can begin very early for talented young people, who are too readily allowed to invest solely in the tag of 'athlete'. The commitment and exclusive dedication perceived as necessary in the pursuit of sporting excellence can restrict the young person's opportunities to engage in behaviours that may be considered *normal* for a child or adolescent.

One missed opportunity is the chance to experiment in a variety of life domains. Experimentation forms the foundation for the child's development of a personal and career identity. Jay Coakley (1992) revealed how young athletes often found it nearly impossible to make commitments to other activities, roles and identities. This lack of experimentation is a concern in desperate need of attention from any coach who is committed to the attainment of sporting excellence and total well-being among his or her athletes.

Physical activity, teamwork and competition at all levels of sport have been cited as essential *life skill* commodities that emerge from a young person's sport participation. However, many existing coaching structures have afforded less attention to other more important commodities, such as self-awareness and self-concept. The consequence has often been a loss of an opportunity to develop the overall person more fully; instead study, social and career achievement have been compromised in the pursuit of sporting excellence. The decision to narrow the young person's life domains is the result of either the demands and expectations of the sport environment or individual choice. In both cases, the responsibility for decision-making is forfeited to adults, such as coaches and parents, highlighting a dependent decision-making style.

Only when the coaching structure can truly comprehend and apply an empowerment approach can we be assured of a far broader development of the athlete, where a recognised goal is to establish emotional intelligence. An empowerment approach is based on a strong sense of self-awareness and impulse control, qualities that are associated with the more exploratory lifestyle of a child whose experience of control and power is far more relaxed. By contrast, in many coaching structures, controlling the environment is deemed paramount to success.

Losing Control Over Your Life and the Implications

In essence, athletes begin to lose control over their lives at a young age and actually lose more control as they develop. From their initial involvement in sport, there exists the potential for children to forfeit all rights of control because they must be willing to be guided by the coach's disciplinary power. Interestingly, in a Canadian study by Werthner and Orlick (1986), 18 of the 28 former Olympic athletes interviewed indicated that they felt they had very little personal control over their lives during their competitive years.

Such findings reflect how young athletes often find themselves in controlled circumstances. The result can be that sport participation becomes a developmental dead-end for them, allowing them no meaningful control over important parts of their lives. Added to this loss of control is the potential for young athletes to openly permit themselves to be controlled through their own self-monitoring processes (e.g. training regimens, dietary requirements), completely neglecting spontaneous existence. Together, these concerns begin to build a strong argument for the promotion of an empowerment approach in coaching.

Rachel Vickery is a New Zealand Commonwealth Games and world championship representative in artistic gymnastics, who retired after the Vancouver Commonwealth Games of 1994. Like most élite representative gymnasts, Rachel commenced gymnastics at a very young age. At eight years of age, she trained four days a week; by the time of the 1990 Auckland Commonwealth Games, when she was 14, she was training 28 to 30 hours per week. The sheer hours of training culminated in a strongly regimented lifestyle, commencing at 5.45 a.m. and concluding at 7.30 p.m., at which time there was an opportunity for dinner, some homework and a 10.30 p.m. bedtime in preparation for the next day's 5.45

a.m. awakening.

Although Rachel readily admits that as a consequence of her gymnastic career she acquired some significant life skills, such as commitment to a goal and persistence, she also indicates the price she paid in relation to her own personal spontaneity:

> Everything was set for us. You had to be there at this time. It was all written down. It was all planned for us. We never really had any choice. Overseas trips—it was never, 'Do you want to go?' It was, 'There's a competition in December. We're going.' Three weeks before my final exam, 'Oh well, you'll just have to study really hard when you get home.' Apparatus-wise we always knew what was expected of us; whether it happened or not was a different story. It was interesting because when we were doing gym everything was controlled for us. I knew where I'd be at 9.30 or whatever. Life was controlled and perfect and rigid.
>
> I was used to having a controlled life, regardless of whether it was me in control or not. It was controlled when I was doing gym, but when I gave up gym, I had all this spare time … What was I going to do? So therefore, I had to control life. I had to be in control of life because there was nobody there in control of my life. It had to be me suddenly. I had to control everything. It wasn't difficult for me. It was difficult for everyone around me because I was so unspontaneous. If I was going to an aerobics class, or whatever, and someone rang and said, 'Look, we're going to the movies, do you want to come?' I'd say, 'Oh no' because I was going to the gym.' I didn't actually tell them that but I wouldn't go because I'd already decided that I was going to the gym—and that was all there was to it.

Research has consistently reported that many young athletes decide to become élite athletes, but from then on parents, coaches and other adults make the decisions. Often these parents and coaches take it upon themselves to guide the young athletes to their goals, which over the long term helps to create and perpetuate social isolation and dependency among these young people.

In 1994, after interviewing seven former American college football players, Kathy Parker concluded that coaches and administrators controlled everything, from the hopes and dreams for the future to the hour-by-hour schedules of the interviewed players. Along similar lines, in interviews for the above-mentioned study by Jay Coakley (1992), 15 adolescent athletes highlighted the pressures and stress related to sport participation; the pressures and stresses that they found to be the worst were those tied to their lack of control over their lives. Athletes frequently referred to the sacrifices they had to make to stay involved in sport and achieve their goals, many of which had been set when they were only 10 or 11 years of age. Coakley concluded that the stress was related to the athlete's lack of control to do things their peers did, to try new things, and to grow in ways unrelated to their sport participation.

In addition to this lack of control by the athlete, research consistently indicates that early participation in sport may heighten status or sense of self, such that in athletic children are viewed and thus treated differently (Krane, Greenleaf & Snow, 1997). Often others strive to keep the day-to-day worries of the world away from the young athlete, presumably to allow that athlete to focus on the sport rather than any external pressures. In this unusual environment, parents and teachers stretch the rules to accommodate the young athlete, who in this way loses vital opportunities to develop and rehearse problem-solving practices.

To this effect, Nicholi (1987) claimed that the internal control absorbed by many adolescents is absent in many young athletes: 'In one sense, athletic development has proceeded at the expense of emotional development' (p.1096). That is, although involvement in sport is frequently credited with the establishment of qualities perceived to be desirable, such as teamwork and competition, the reality may be that sufficient attention is not given to the true qualities required for emotional development—qualities such as self-awareness, impulse control, motivation, empathy and social deftness, which mark people who excel in relationships and the workplace.

Clearly, it is pertinent to ask when this artificial and protected world becomes more damaging than helpful for the athlete. The hindered emotional development, the general lack of development in areas other than sport, and the unbalanced perception of the world are liabilities that can become critical when the young person concludes the athlete role and must redefine the sense of self. Significantly, Rachel Vickery relates a conflict with her own expression of emotion in her life after gymnastics. The conflict was associated with both her inability to identify emotion and so to regulate this emotion for her own mental well-being:

> You walk through those doors and you can't have emotions. That was another thing I had to train myself really hard to do—to be able to express emotion. In the gym you either had tears or negativity, but not really anything else. We were like robots in the end. You never had time to think about anything that happened in the rest of your life, except gym. Even when you got home at night and you'd had a bad session that dictated the mood you took home, and even through the weekend. It didn't matter that you might have had a good day at school. Who cares if you got an 'A', you still fell off the beam five times and couldn't stick any routines ...
>
> I went to the orthopaedic surgeon 10 days after I'd been discharged [from hospital, after breaking a leg]. And it was then that the whole reality hit ... I can't drive for three months. I had a really good cry—a good cry for me lasts about

three minutes—and that was the first time Mum had ever seen me cry like that because normally I wouldn't allow myself to do it. Again, it's taken me four years to be able to do that.

The athlete's strong identification with sport invariably begins in childhood, and intensifies through the developmental and adult years. Research has consistently suggested that children enjoy sports because of the potential for:

- improving skills;
- having fun;
- playing with friends;
- experiencing certain thrills and pleasures;
- achieving and maintaining a level of fitness; and
- achieving success in a socially desirable realm (Gould & Horn, 1984).

It is noteworthy that the degree to which children enjoy sport almost always appears as one of their primary reasons for participating or dropping out. Thus coaches must surely have a responsibility to recognise that their young athletes may be seeking to fulfil any number of the above needs. In reality, however, many children experience a coaching environment that overemphasises physical activity and competition. Little regard is given to independent personal development, which underpins an empowerment approach and is frequently cited by children as paramount to their enjoyment in sport.

Athlete Identity

In contrast to the motives for participation as a child, young elite athletes burn out and leave competitive sport because of:

- a constrained set of life experiences leading to the development of a one-dimensional self-concept; and
- power relationships in and around sport that seriously restrict the young athlete's control over their lives (Coakley, 1992).

Young people who experience both conditions are likely to be highly accomplished athletes who have been heavily involved in a single sport for relatively long periods. Their sport participation often involves social experiences that foster the development of a single identity exclusively related to sport participation and perpetuates a limited set of social relationships directly tied to sport. The people in their lives continuously respond to them in terms of their specialised sport roles. Their time is almost exclusively devoted to the development of specialised skills, and their goals are well defined and tied to assumptions of commitment to long-term specialised sport training. As Rachel describes:

> I don't think I ever knew who I was when I was doing gym. I had a personality and I was a person, but I don't think it was ever really me. I was the one at Rangitoto College who was a gymnast. In a way I was even more known as 'Rachel the Gymnast'. In a way that was a pressure. Teachers who didn't know would get to know me as 'Rachel the Gymnast'. It didn't worry me—in a way it worked in my favour. I never had an extension on any assignment, but I always knew I could've if I needed it.

Research has consistently reported that talented young athletes direct so much mental energy toward sports that their self-esteem becomes based on athletic performance. That is, little energy remains for other areas of personal development. They focus on sports 'often to the neglect of education and participation in other social domains' (Nicholi, 1987, p. 128). Consequently, when the prospect of retirement looms, it is more than an event for which the athlete is completely unprepared; it may pose a serious threat to their very identity. As McPherson (1980) stated:

> The athlete experiences this loss of self-respect and the need to be socially significant. In the case of the athlete, the problem is more critical because he or she has become accustomed to living in the public eye and because retirement before 35 years of age is not normally socially sanctioned (p. 130).

Chris Nicholson is a triple Olympian: he competed in the Barcelona Olympic Games 100-kilometre cycling time-trial, as well as skating at the Albertville and Lillehammer Winter Olympic Games. From his initial experiences of sport he developed a clear athletic identity at a very young age. Based on this identity, Chris assumed an exclusive dedication was necessary to his achievement in sport, meaning that he failed to pursue other significant life domains such as education and career. Yet by the time of his preparatory phase leading up to the Lillehammer Winter Olympic Games of 1994, there were many broader influences in his life—he was newly married, working full time and studying part time. Chris looks back on his perspective as a young athlete:

> In terms of performing well in my sport, what I should've done would've been some tertiary education when I left school and done a little bit of skating when it fitted in. I got to 25, or whatever, and I was thinking, 'Well what am I going to do for the rest of my life?' I started to think on those lines, and that's when my body was getting right. I burned out so much of that mental energy and enthusiasm and sacrifice and commitment and all that, when I was 17, 18 and 19. So there wasn't that much there [later on], and also it shut down the opportunities.
>
> I didn't stop to think, 'Five years from now I want to actually have a job'. The lure of being able to get some kind of qualifications so I could work because I was sold out to the idea that sport was the medium. I hadn't thought it through

like that and so because I was thinking in the immediate term, 'I want to do next years world champs', I was thinking that I have to earn what I can now to save up the money for the fare. So I was thinking short-term. So I lost the tertiary education opportunities.

Further investigation into Chris's unique circumstances reveals a young athlete whose self-worth was entirely linked to his athletic performance: 'I was selling out to the principle that skating faster is the way to become a full person. Your value as a person is measured by your lap time.'

If a child is internally and externally rewarded for developing a multiplicity of skills and interests, the individual's self-worth will not depend solely on success in one role. However, if the child's athlete identity is reinforced to the exclusion of other facets of his or her personality, then self-worth will be almost totally contingent upon success or failure as an athlete. Unfortunately, too many adults responsible for junior sport programmes adhere to the philosophy that success in sport can only be realised in an environment of total sporting focus, with little if any regard for the concurrent development of vital social and educational skills. Rachel describes her experience of such an environment:

You get stuck with the thought that you have to be committed. It's the whole commitment thing, and if you want to be an élite sportsperson you have to be committed, so if you're told that you train, and you don't want to or you can't, it's like you're not showing commitment, so therefore you're less likely to achieve. I wanted to be a top gymnast, so you just learnt to put up with everything that goes with it. You accept that that's the norm ...

In '94, I started to think, 'Why am I really doing this?' The other thing, when you're on that treadmill—gym, school, gym—you never get the time to sit back and question it. You're so exhausted—you're either doing your schoolwork or you're at the gym. You didn't actually make the decision, 'I definitely want this' or 'It's a real drag'. You don't enjoy it as much as you would if you had a more holistic life. I think that would have a good effect on your performance. Sure, [in the environment of total sport focus] you're there and 100 per cent committed, but mentally it's still, 'Oh, oh, I have to be at training'.

Among young élite athletes experiencing this career crisis, such as both Chris and Rachel, the emotional and other psychological responses are nearly universal. Therefore coaches must be encouraged to recognise, acknowledge and appreciate effort and emotion in their young athletes, as is consistent with an empowerment approach to coaching, where athletes take ownership for their sport and life. Coaches must also recognise that effort and emotion are transferable commodities, and form the cornerstone of development in all spheres of human endeavour, including social life, education and career.

It is worth drawing attention to an additional comment from Chris concerning his lack of career planning. He claims that such planning would be perceived as a threat to his athletic career: 'If anything interfered with the training programme, you just didn't do it.'

It is clear that individuals with a strong and exclusive commitment to the athlete role are likely to be less prepared for a post-sport career than individuals who have invested less in the role. It is critical that athletes are made aware that their sport involvement will not last forever. In accordance with Chris Nicholson's comment, it must be recognised that many young athletes lack either the time or interest to engage in any form of career planning. These young athletes view such planning as a threat to their athletic identity and dream of being a professional athlete.

This perception of threat highlights the need for every endeavour to be made to promote a sense of motivation, self-awareness and self-regulation in all young athletes. One contribution to this end is to introduce training diaries that emphasise the setting of weekly goals not only for technical skills, but also in mental and life skill development. In addition, coaches must readily express their interest in the whole person, rather than just the athletic component of the person, by constantly questioning the young athlete on matters relating to study and social accomplishment, as well as physical skill development.

Present day New Zealand is being forced into recognising the implications of sport professionalism. Like never before in our history, high school students foresee a possibility of a professional career in sport. Significantly, focus on athletic excellence is frequently leading to a foreclosure of other roles, whereby important life domains such as career, education and social development, along with cognitive skills in decision making and problem solving, are tragically neglected. That is, young, potentially élite athletes who invest in revenue-producing sports may be unprepared to take advantage of the most valued aspects of their high school days— the initiation and development of social skills and viable vocational plans.

Coakley (1992) reported that most of the young athletes interviewed began to wonder if they were giving up too many activities and experiences that seemed very important in the lives of their peers. Along similar lines, a study of a former élite gymnast, conducted by Krane, Greenleaf and Snow (1997), revealed that the emphasis on winning overshadowed many more ordinary concerns such as fun, social interactions with peers and healthy parent–child relationships. Krane, Greenleaf and Snow concluded that this type of behaviour might lead to many maladaptive behaviours and mental states:

It seems that Susan and her parents were socialised to believe that these excessive training techniques were a necessary aspect of elite sport performance. Without being presented with an alternative training perspective, they obediently subscribed to techniques of these 'highly successful' elite level coaches (p. 59).

Implications for Coaches

It is important for significantly involved adults to help young talented athletes to understand the nature of a role in sports and competition. Coaches must ensure that the child's self-worth is not solely dependent upon winning or losing, by promoting a more effort-based reward structure. Children tend to experience judgements of their athletic ability as direct reflections on their total worth as people. Therefore, if children are exposed to social rejection or humiliation as a response to athletic performance, self-doubt and low self-esteem may become engrained in their character. It is essential that coaches who work at this level teach young athletes to put athletics and athletic prowess in the proper perspective, and assist young athletes to transfer emotional skills into other domains of life. A coach who understands an empowerment approach and implements it in their coaching structure will open up an opportunity for young athletes to accomplish this emotional development.

Quite simply, winning strategies are only part of a coach's obligations. Cultivating communicative relationships with their athletes and providing for their personal development are vital, yet often neglected necessities. Coakley (1992) identified an ideological assumption that high-performance sport programmes have been organised to produce performance outcomes rather than opportunities for overall social development and critical self-assessment of how sport participation is tied to the wider lives of young athletes. In accordance with an empowerment philosophy, by failing to give the athlete information or to take the time to explain what is happening or what the options are, a coach deprives that athlete of the opportunity to promote his or her own sense of control. In their discussion of the coach's obligations, Thomas and Ermler (1988) noted:

> The coach and other managers in the athletic establishment have traditionally remained the autocratic centre of the athlete's world. Retaining the knowledge, control and ultimate responsibility for the athlete's world is often justified in order to achieve outcome objectives. It is the sincere, often altruistic belief of the coaching establishment that a favour is being done for the athlete of whom they have charge by taking care of details, making the decisions, and literally spoiling the athlete so that his or her full attention can be directed to the quest for athletic excellence (p. 139).

In accordance with an empowerment approach, coaches should provide feedback that will assist the athlete towards self-awareness. That is, they should extend feedback statements beyond those utilised for physical skill performance, to include emotional skills such as identifying, labelling and expressing feelings and controlling impulses. They should reward young athletes for demonstrating the use of steps in problem solving and decision making, understanding the perspective of others and developing realistic expectations about themselves. Any young athlete who recognises the value of these emotional skills will be become less likely to associate their entire self-worth with athletic performance.

Promoting a strong sense of self-awareness is essential to a coaching approach that develops a whole-person, and is a vital component of the empowerment approach advocated in this book. Through questioning (see Chapter Eight), a coach can overcome many of the issues related to the dysfunctional aspects of an athletic identity. Through the development of cognitive skills in problem solving and decision making, the young athletes will build up vital life skills such as the regulation of motivational self-statements, positive inner dialogue, empathy toward others and social acceptance. It is upon the realisation of these qualities, through carefully planned and structured coaching environments, that coaches will gain both results on the field of play and satisfaction in the knowledge that they have promoted better people and not just better athletes.

Coaches must strive to encourage and reinforce the independence of young athletes, and continually emphasise their personal responsibility. Athletes must play an active role in all decision making, with coaches resisting the temptation to take charge throughout difficult times. Rather than stretching the rules of life to accommodate young athletes, coaches should expose them to the normal day-to-day worries of the world in which they live.

Learning how to empower your athletes is a vital coaching skill. To date, it has been afforded far too little attention in the promotion of coach education. Yet with an empowerment approach, athletes can acquire essential problem-solving and action-planning abilities that will transcend the sporting field and spill over into their overall success as people both immediately and in the long term.

Too often we give children answers to remember rather than problems to solve.

—Roger Lewin, US humorist, author

References

Coakley, J.J. (1992). Burnout among adolescent athletes: a personal failure or social problem?, *Sociology of Sport Journal, 9,* 271–285.

Gould, D., & Horn, T.S. (1984). Participation motivation in young athletes. In J.M. Silva & R.S. Weinberg (eds), *Psychological Foundations of Sports,* pp. 359–370. Champaign, IL: Human Kinetics.

Krane, V., Greenleaf, C.A., & Snow, J. (1997). Reaching for gold and the price of glory: a motivational case study of an elite gymnast, *The Sport Psychologist, 11*(1), 53–71.

McPherson, B.D. (1980). Retirement from professional sport: the process and problems of occupational and psychological adjustment, *Sociological Symposium, 30,* 126–143.

Nicholi, A.M. (1987). Psychiatric consultation in professional football, *New England Journal of Medicine, 316,* 1095–1100.

Parker, K. (1994). 'Has-beens' and 'wanna-bes': Transition experiences of former major college football players, *The Sport Psychologist, 8*(3), 287–304.

Thomas, C.E., & Ermler, K.L. (1988). Institutional obligations in the athletic retirement process, *Quest, 40,* 137–150.

Werthner, P., & Orlick, T. (1986). Retirement experiences of successful Olympic athletes, *International Journal of Sport Psychology, 17,* 337–363.

Chapter Eight

Asking the right questions takes as
much skill as giving the right answers.

—Robert Half

Asking Meaningful Questions[1]

In Chapters Three, Four and Six all the coaches and athletes interviewed sent a clear message about taking an empowerment approach to coaching: it is important to ask meaningful questions. When coaches ask questions, athletes must find answers, which in turn increases their knowledge and understanding of the purpose of particular skill performances and tactical plays in the context of competition. As John Dewey has said, 'Thinking in itself is questioning'. Questioning stimulates athletes' thinking, providing them a chance to be creative and make decisions. It is also an extremely powerful means to inspire in athletes an intrinsic motivation to learn.

An empowering coaching approach is ineffectual without a high level of questioning and clarifying to generate answers from the athletes. It is known that athletes learn well and have higher retention rates (see Chapter Two) if they are given the opportunity to work out for themselves what to do and how to do it. As part of becoming empowering coaches, we need to learn to apply an effective questioning technique at training sessions, to enhance athlete learning.

As Robyn Jones mentioned in Chapter Five, implementing an empowerment approach and using questioning may be uncommon and, to some, may feel unnatural. Athletes may initially be surprised that they can have input into solving problems and thus their immediate response may not be favourable. However, if questioning becomes part of a coach's repertoire, and the coach focuses on questioning well, then athletes will enjoy solving problems and be successful.

Among advocates of a prescriptive coaching approach, there is a perception that coaches who ask questions do not know the answers themselves. Indeed, coaches may find it difficult, and at times daunting, to design questions that generate high-level thinking from the athletes. Yet

---

[1] A large portion of this chapter is adapted from Chapter 6 in Kidman, L., & Hanrahan, S.J. (1997). *The Coaching Process: A Practical Guide to Improving Your Effectiveness.* Palmerston North: Dunmore. Permission has been granted.

to create situations where athletes learn best, by listening to their responses, then redirecting, prompting or probing for better or more complete answers, coaches must have an in-depth understanding of the material they are asking about and the context in which it will be applied. As Wayne Smith suggests:

> To truly empower athletes to take responsibility for their learning, use game specific activities, ensure that they have fun and use questioning for them to become self-aware … I believe at the élite level, the questioning approach really tests your knowledge and in particular your eyes and technical nous.

When coaches pose questions athletes will try hard to solve a problem if given the opportunity. The solution they generate is theirs and thus athletes will take ownership and remember, understand and apply the content more effectively than if they were told what to do, when to do it and how to do it. Solving problems through coach questioning enables athletes to explore, discover, create and generally experiment with a variety of moving and tactical processes of a specific sport.

Sport and physical activity are superb ways to involve athletes in high-level thinking. Coaches need to test out their questioning strategy in each particular situation and adapt it to meet the purpose of the training session and athletes' needs and expectations. Coaches are often surprised and excited by how much athletes really do know and how easily they self-learn.

Questions to Promote Low-order and High-order Thinking

The goals of effective questioning include actively involving athletes in the learning process, and enhancing their task mastery and conceptual understanding. Another goal is to promote both simple (low-order) and complex (high-order) thinking. These two forms of thinking require different types of questions.

When athletes need to remember specific ideas or concepts, *simple* or *low-order questions* are appropriate. These questions serve as reminder cues that might be important to a learning sequence. Low-order questions are often *what?* or *where?* questions asked during drills. Low-order questions are factual, generally with only one possible answer. Examples of low-order questions used in coaching are:

- 'What part of the foot do you use to kick a goal?'

- 'Where should you aim when shooting in netball?'

- 'What is the lunge in fencing?'

- 'Who is the captain of the New Zealand women's hockey team?'

Research indicates that coaches tend to use low-order questions and certainly in some instances low-order questions are appropriate. However, coaches should strive to ask more *high-order questions* to extend athletes' opportunities to self-evaluate.

High-order questions require abstract or higher-level thinking processes. These questions challenge athletes to apply, analyse, synthesise, evaluate and create knowledge. They are generally more appropriate for analysing tactics and complex skills. Although both children and élite athletes respond well to high-order questions, it is advantageous for coaches to create the questions according to the athletes' developmental needs. Designing high-order questions and questioning sequence is more appropriate when encouraging independent learning, where athletes are required to think in greater depth about the subject matter or context and can search for multiple answers. Examples of high-order questions in sport settings include:

·   'How can we get the ball down the court quickly?'

·   'In how many different ways can you balance on the balance beam?'

·   'How can you get around the defence?'

·   'Why should we push the defence to the sideline?'

·   'Why do we need to tuck when doing a somersault?'

Why? and *how?* questions enhance athletes' ability to make decisions, one of the central goals of empowerment emphasised in earlier chapters. It is important for coaches to allow athletes to think about questions and help and encourage them to answer. If athletes are having difficulty with the answer, a coach can redirect or rephrase a high-order question so they can think carefully about what has been asked. However, the coach should never give the answer itself, as it takes ownership of the problem-solving process away from the athletes.

With high-order questions, there are no 'wrong' answers as the athletes generally interpret the questions at their own level of understanding. Coaches need to listen closely to the answers, interpret the significance and respond accordingly. Often athletes come up with answers that coaches may find useful to elaborate and apply within their game plan. By listening, in other words, coaches can learn much from their athletes.

Tactical questioning and technique questioning are two specific kinds of high-order questions that can be very helpful to the empowering coach. Both strategies are detailed below, before consideration is given to a third strategy that forms a useful part of high-order questioning: movement response.

Tactical questioning

Questions that call for decision making and problem solving with re-spect to the strategies of the competition are tactical questions. Prescrip-tive coaches often direct and decide on the competition plan. Yet unless athletes understand why the game plan exists and take ownership of it, then coaches will find it difficult for athletes to accept and understand it. To increase tactical awareness and decision making, coaches should use many high-order questions that allow athletes to create and develop their ideas.

In an empowerment approach, coaches set up tactical situations as problem-solving exercises. They then ask *how?* and *why?* questions to solve tactical problems and enhance understanding. Examples of some useful questions might be, 'Given a three-on-two situation, where is the space? Why?' or 'How would you finish the race in the last 100 metres?' It is important for the athletes to perform the actual movement so they solve problems, seek solutions through practice and try various alterna-tives, and thus build a better understanding of variable situations.

Technique questioning

Formulating questions for athletes to become aware of their technique helps to provide them with purposeful feedback. Through this mecha-nism, coaches prompt athletes and compare their actions to an ideal model of performance. Hadfield (1994) introduced this method as the 'query theory', which Kidman and Hadfield (2000, p. 14) have summarised as follows:

> While words are different to bodily feelings and are associated with different parts of the brain, athletes must answer questions (such as 'what happened to your hips when you played that shot?') based on knowledge and understanding passed to their brain by their proprioceptive sensors. The basis of this approach is to increase kinaesthetic (body and sensory) awareness of appropriate skill execution and be able to make decisions about what strengths to keep and what weaknesses to fix (and how to fix it). In plain language, if athletes cannot feel it, they cannot change it.

To help the athletes gain kinaesthetic awareness, a coach uses demon-strations that provide them with mental images. The athletes then ex-ecute the skill based on their own knowledge and existing motor pro-gramme. In the process of skill execution, the coach observes and analy-ses the athletes and identifies strengths and weaknesses.

To aid the athletes in comparing their action with the ideal model, the coach asks *what?, where?, why?* and *how?* questions (e.g. 'What did your arms do when you released the ball?', 'Where was your head when the hockey stick contacted the ball?', 'Why is it important to have a follow through?', 'How did your legs move to complete the handspring?'). These types of questions should help athletes become self-aware of their body movements in executing a skill. If athletes are still unaware of what their bodies are doing, the coach can use 'shaping' questions (e.g. 'What did the demonstration show you about using your legs?', 'How did you use your legs?').

Next the athletes execute the technique using their knowledge and kinaesthetic awareness. At this stage, the coach should allow the athletes to experience the technique several times before asking another question. The purpose of such sequences is to enable the athletes to become self-aware of the technique and to take responsibility for making decisions. In this way, when they are performing the technique in a competition, the athletes can understand how to perform it and when it feels right.

Movement responses

Although questioning has always been considered a mental strategy, athletes can learn much through problem solving and questioning using movement responses. A movement response requires an answer that involves a physical demonstration.

A typical example of a problem that requires movement response is, 'Show us how to control the ball most effectively' or 'Show me how to grip the racquet'. Even though the coach does not express either of these statements as a question, the athletes must provide answers by showing the coach how they understand.

Posing movement questions is an effective tool to enhance physical skill learning. In providing movement responses, athletes can identify faults or determine correct skill technique. Consistent with the query theory, if athletes have input into correcting skill performance, with appropriate self-awareness, they tend to retain the information they have discovered. Through this mechanism, some athletes may determine the correction they need for a technique that their coach has been trying to correct in them for years.

A note on rhetorical questions

Coaches should avoid using *rhetorical questions.* A rhetorical question is one that coaches do not expect athletes to answer or that coaches answer themselves. An example is, 'Can you please pick up that baton?' The response might be, 'No, I can't ...' Other examples are when the coach asks, 'Will you please sit down?' but is actually giving a direction, or asks, 'What is the best way best way to pass to another player?' then gives the answer, encouraging the athletes to be passive.

Techniques for Effective Questioning

Questions are only as good as the answers they extract. What follows are some useful tips to enhance coaches' questioning skills.

Planning questions

Formulating meaningful questions is a key element in establishing a great questioning environment. Planning the questions for the training session ahead is the most important step, especially if questioning is a very new part of the coaching repertoire. As noted in Chapter Three, Wayne Smith encourages such planning:

> On my practice plan, I have questions, general questions that I would be asking them. Like the decision, where I saw [someone] in an attacking situation that didn't pass the ball, 'What did you do, what did you see, why didn't you pass it?'—basically to get feedback and ensure they were developing self-awareness about skill execution and tactical understanding.

To plan meaningful, clear and coherent questions, an empowering coach will:

- consider the nature of the content to be mastered and the athletes' readiness to contribute;

- practise the questions for the next training session by writing them down;

- ensure there is a variety of high and low-order questions;

- ensure there is an answer to work towards (and know the answer), with the questions planned to lead systematically to the planned answer; and

- formulate the questions appropriate to the athletes' level of learning by reading the questions aloud (e.g. 'What flight angle will be most appropriate to get the ball through the goal post?' may not suit athletes under the age of six).

For example, a coach's goal may be for the athletes to learn the footwork involved in a bowl in tenpin bowling. The coach would like the athletes to find out what the steps might be. Before starting to question, the coach determines the steps up the bowling lane to where the ball is released. Then he or she begins to create the questions. The first question might be, 'If you were to release the ball at the boundary line, which foot would have to be in the front?' Once the athletes have worked out the answer, the coach might ask, 'How many steps would it take to get to the line where you release the ball?' The next question might be, 'So if it takes three steps to the release line, what should your foot position be at the start?' The athletes will give many different answers, but each of them will work out the answer in his or her own way. By the end of the set of questions, athletes will have solved the problem about their footwork, with no instruction from the coach.

In planning questions, it is also important to be flexible in both developing the questions and timing the questions. Among coaches who are new to questioning, it is common to ask the planned questions but not to move beyond those questions in the training session. However, the real art of questioning is to read the athletes, look at what is happening and ask relevant questions when the athletes are ready or need to solve a problem. For example, Wayne Smith plans general questions, then in training he formulates further meaningful questions based on the situation as he reads it.

After implementing the questioning strategy, coaches should evaluate the session to improve their questioning skills. To this end, they may write down questions used and determine their relevance, or get someone on the sideline to evaluate these questions.

Gain the athletes' attention

An important management strategy in questioning is to ensure that all athletes are quiet and listening to the questioning sequence. To this end, a coach may create rules to encourage attention. Useful examples of rules include, 'When one person is talking, everyone else listens' or 'Raise your hand and wait to be called on'. Notice that to contribute to a supportive environment, both rules contain positive words, rather than negative words like 'Don't'.

Once the coach has the attention of all athletes, everyone can hear the questions, while the coach can make appropriate eye contact and look for nonverbal signs of misunderstanding or excitement among the athletes. At this stage, the coach can begin the planned segment using questioning strategies.

When is it appropriate to ask questions?

An issue Wayne Smith raises is the need to choose the right moment for athletes to solve problems. The ability to pick this moment is considered part of the art of coaching. When Wayne first implemented his empowering approach, he noted that he often overquestioned in his enthusiasm to get athletes to take responsibility.

There is no formula for the right time to ask questions. The answer is, 'It depends'. It depends on fatigue, it depends on 'teachable moments', it depends on intrinsic motivation and it depends on whether the athlete has managed to solve the problem by himself or herself. A coach should read or analyse each situation to determine if the athletes need to solve a problem at that time and in that situation. Often coaches jump in because they feel like they are not doing anything and need to advise. More often athletes can determine their own mistakes and fix them because of their own decision-making ability and self-awareness. When an athlete makes a mistake and obviously knows it, there is nothing so stressful as being reminded of it by some significant other.

Athletes are bright; coaches should allow them to determine their needs and have faith in their ability to solve problems. As Rene Deleplace said, 'There is no point in coaching unless the teaching you do helps the student to overtake you.'

Wait time

One of the reasons for gaining and maintaining athletes' attention is to provide wait time for athletes to consider their responses to the question. Increasing wait time enables athletes to formulate better responses and encourages athletes to give longer answers because they have had the opportunity to think. When given this 'thinking time', athletes tend to volunteer more appropriate answers and are less likely to fail to respond. They are more able to respond to high-order questions because they tend to speculate more. With longer wait time, athletes tend to ask more questions in return. If they do not understand or they need to find out more information, athletes also feel they have been given an opportunity to clarify the question. With longer wait time, athletes exhibit more confidence in their comments and those athletes whom coaches rate as relatively slow learners offer more questions and more responses.

Wait time is quite difficult for coaches when they are first learning how to question. Research on teaching suggests that teachers tend to answer their own questions when a wrong answer is given or tend to become impatient. As in teaching, an appropriate wait time in coaching is three to five seconds. Once they have mastered wait time, coaches will find that athletes benefit more from questioning than they do if the coach calls on them for an immediate response.

To increase wait time, an empowering coach will:

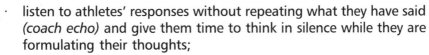
- listen to athletes' responses without repeating what they have said *(coach echo)* and give them time to think in silence while they are formulating their thoughts;

· be careful not to call an athlete's name immediately after posing the question. Once the coach identifies an athlete to answer the question, the other athletes tend to relax and discontinue their thinking process;

· show he or she is listening by limiting comments and being aware of using 'uh-huh' and 'okay';

· avoid a 'Yes but ...' reaction to an athlete's response, which signals that coach rejects the athlete's idea; and

· allow the athletes to provide the answers.

Reinforcement

As athletes offer solutions, either verbally or through a movement response, a coach should encourage their innovative ideas—no matter how silly or inadequate the coach may perceive those ideas to be. If they find no sincere support for answers (either verbal or nonverbal), the athletes will be less likely to respond next time they are questioned. If someone were to offer an answer to which the response was, 'What a stupid answer', how would the athlete feel? Would the athlete feel that the coach has demonstrated respect for him or her? Would the athlete (and perhaps other athletes who have seen how their answers may be treated) be likely to volunteer an answer next time? Thus part of the process of questioning is to encourage athletes to continue to try for a solution, even though they may appear to be a long way from it.

In Chapter Five, Robyn Jones highlights the importance of establishing an environment in which athletes feel confident to volunteer responses. The difficulty here, when a coach is deciding how to handle an inadequate answer, is to determine whether the athlete is off task or deliberately trying to be silly. If the response is off task, the coach should refocus or ignore it, then reinforce the athlete's next attempt to respond. Sincere positive reinforcement will be more likely to motivate athletes to respond enthusiastically to later questions. It is also noted that different individuals respond to different types of reinforcement.

For effective reinforcement, an empowering coach will:

· praise based on the athlete's answer—for example, 'That's an interesting answer, can you tell us why you said that?';

· praise with the focus on reinforcing the athlete's response;

· praise honestly and sincerely; and

· give nonverbal reinforcement such as eye contact, thumbs up, smiling, nodding, and clapping hands—all extremely useful as forms of praise.

Prompting

With prompting, coaches use cues to 'remind' athletes of something that they have learned and help them to answer a question. Examples are, 'What did you determine about using a fake on offence?' or 'How have you been putting the shuttlecock on the floor? Think about the racquet swing.'

It is important that in giving cues, coaches do not give athletes the whole answer. The purpose of prompting is to encourage athletes to provide a response. Prompting can help them gain the confidence to answer the question.

Probing

Probing is a questioning strategy in which a coach asks follow-up questions so that athletes can extend, amplify or refine their answers. Here the coach should avoid using 'uh-huh's or 'okay's as these comments show a lack of interest in athletes' responses.

The following is an example of an effective probing sequence.

Coach: 'How can we get the ball down the court?'

Athlete: 'Dribble it.'

Coach: 'Is there a way you can get it down faster?' *(probe)*

Athlete: 'You could run faster.'

Coach: 'That is a good answer. What other skill have we been learning to move the ball around?' *(probe)*

Athlete: 'Passing.'

Coach: 'Great. Now what is it about passing the ball that gets the ball down the court faster?' *(probe)*

Athlete: 'When you pass the ball to a person, the speed of the ball is faster than when you dribble.'

Coach: 'Now you are getting the idea. If the ball is faster when passing, what does that mean when you are being defended?' *(probe)*

Athlete: 'The defender has less time to recover when you pass the ball to someone else. When you dribble, the ball is moved more slowly and therefore the defender has more time to catch up.'

Probing and reinforcing promote learning through extending current thought processes and encouraging athletes' responses.

Equity of directing and distributing questions

Coaches will notice that some athletes cannot wait to answer the questions while others prefer to remain anonymous in the background. The athletes who volunteer readily are probably the most confident in their skills and their cognitive abilities. Research in teaching suggests that the teacher tends to neglect the students in the back. This same tendency will be found in sport settings as well. Coaches must make a conscious effort to include all members of the team/squad in problem solving.

Coaches should allow equal time for all athletes to contribute to the discussion. Through skilful directing and distributing of discussion, they will provide a fair environment where athletes can contribute equally. Directing questions to athletes in a nonthreatening way can encourage those who still may not be prone to participate. If a reluctant participant responds to a question, the coach should praise this answer and use the content of the response in further discussion.

Guided discovery of a new skill

Many coaches believe that they must tell and show their athletes exactly how to perform a correct technique. In contrast, through Game Sense (see Chapter Two) athletes learn technique through guided discovery (and through self-awareness). The coach gives guidance with a series of meaningful questions about the athlete's technique (while recognising that athletes are capable of participating in sport without being taught the perfect technique). Athletes then learn by discovering how to do the technique themselves, in a process similar to the query theory, but learning is a result of self-discovery, rather than watching a demonstration.

Techniques do not have to be taught explicitly as athletes at all levels can often 'figure out' the approach needed. A good example is found by observing children in action in the playground, where they are very capable of discovering how to perform the 'game' without being told by someone else.

To use guided discovery as a coaching tool, it is useful to plan the line of inquiry. The coach should first decide and plan the answer or ultimate technique, then arrange the questions for the athletes to discover the answer. Athletes then provide demonstrations of the techniques as they discover the solution.

This process may be illustrated through the following example, in which athletes discover how to find the open space after a dribble in soccer.

Coach: 'In a three-on-three situation, what is the best way to get the ball to your teammate? Let's try it.'

Athletes pass all kinds of different ways.

Coach: 'What happens if you pass the ball behind your teammate? Let's try it.'

Athletes pass to partners and aim everywhere. Some athletes have to turn around and run for the ball, some are going forward nicely.

Coach: 'Now, if you want to make sure that your teammate goes forward (towards the goal), where do you want the pass to go?'

Johnny: 'They should go behind the person.'

Coach: 'Great, let's see how that works, Johnny. All go out in your threes and try to pass behind the person'.

The athletes try this approach.

Coach: 'Did that work?'

Athletes: (In unison) 'No!!'

Coach: 'Why didn't it work?'

Athletes: 'Because we had to keep coming backwards.'

Coach: 'So how shall we do it this time?'

Kirsten: 'We should pass it to the front of the player.'

Coach: 'Great, let's try what Kirsten said.'

From this step the coach might get the athletes to practise in a game, concentrating on passing forward or passing to the place where the athletes are headed. After the athletes have mastered the concept, the coach might call them in again and try the same sort of discovery for passing and running to a space. An example might be, 'Now that we can pass it well, what do you think the player who just passed the ball should do?'

Notice that in the above example, the coach never provides an explanation or demonstration. Instead, the athletes figure out for themselves how to pass forward. With any method where athletes have to figure out how a technique is performed, they will not only retain and understand that technique more fully, but also get more practice opportunities and take control of their own technique experience. Athletes tend to remember more because they are doing it, rather than watching a coach explain and demonstrate.

Conclusion

Asking meaningful questions can give coaches a huge advantage in applying the empowerment approach. This chapter has highlighted some useful techniques to ensure their questions are meaningful. It is important for coaches to realise that it takes plenty of practice to use meaningful questions in a purposeful way. Moreover, coaches who use questioning well will enjoy it for the rewards it brings. While they need to be aware of the considerations that should shape the way they use meaningful questions (see Chapter Five), they can also be aware of how athletes will benefit from being able to work out problems, discover their own abilities and make informed decisions. The use of effective questioning will further enhance a coach's repertoire and promote their athletes' learning.

References

Hadfield, D.C. (1994). The query theory: a sports coaching model for the 90's, *The New Zealand Coach, 3*(4), 16–20.

Kidman, L., & Hadfield, D. (2000). Athlete empowerment, *New Zealand Coach, 8*(4), 14–15.

*One who is afraid of asking questions
is ashamed of learning.*

—*Danish Proverb*

*He who asks questions cannot
avoid the answers.*

—*Cameroonian Proverb*

Chapter Nine   *If only the sun-drenched celebrities are being noticed and worshipped, then our children are going to have a tough time seeing the value in the shadows, where the thinkers, probers and scientists are keeping society together.*

—Rita Dove, US poet, educator

Children and Sport

Children learn what they live
Children who live with criticism, learn to condemn.
Children who live with hostility, learn to fight.
Children who live with ridicule, learn to be shy.
Children who live with shame, learn to feel guilty.
Children who live with tolerance, learn to be patient.
Children who live with encouragement, learn confidence.
Children who live with praise, learn to appreciate.
Children who live with fairness, learn justice.
Children who live with approval, learn to like themselves.
Children who live with acceptance and friendship, learn to find love in the world.

— Anonymous

As the folk wisdom above richly illustrates, children learn what they live. This chapter complements the analysis of Teaching Games for Understanding in Chapter Two, by discussing the influences on children's learning and participation in sport.

Children are motivated and learn well when coaches use an empowering approach (including Teaching Games for Understanding). As discussed in previous chapters, children learn by making their own decisions and through trial and error. Potentially, sport can offer them the opportunity to demonstrate flair and experience excitement. However, coaches (and other adults, such as parents) are notorious for taking decisions away from children by telling them what to do and when to do it, with an emphasis on robotic plays and perfecting technique (see Rod Thorpe's discussion of technique and games in Chapter Two).

There are a multitude of reasons why children participate in sport. Many children are prompted to start sport by suggestions or influence from their parents or other adults (Roberts, Treasure & Hall, 1994). While it is important for adults to support their children and encourage them to participate in sport, they should be careful to keep children's motives in the foreground. The adult-structured sport organisation and the pressure adults can put on children increase stress, which in turn can increase the risk that children will leave sport. Ultimately, recognising that children are the future in sport, adults must enable children to learn and experience success in their own terms, so they continue to enjoy and thrive in sport.

These issues are examined in more detail in this chapter. Discussed first are the benefits and disadvantages of competition for children. The chapter then moves on to the reasons why children participate in sport and why many drop out. Thereafter it addresses the kinds of pressure adults put on children in sport and the influence of comments that adults make in the 'heat of the moment' on the sideline during children's competition. The chapter concludes with a look at the importance of ensuring that children experience a balanced lifestyle, in which sport is only a part of their life.

Children and Competition

Traditionally, sport has been considered a means by which children can learn values and discipline, as well as develop morally and socially (e.g. skills in teamwork and cooperation). However, there is a lack of research to show conclusively that participation in organised sport programmes leads to the development of appropriate values and attitudes, morals, or other characteristics traditionally associated with sport involvement (Coakley, 1992). To the contrary, in many recorded instances sport has been shown to teach inappropriate values and attitudes (i.e. cheating and violence).

Thus sport involvement does not necessarily equal positive socialisation. Rather, significant others, including adults and coaches, contribute to the building of character and moral development, both positively and negatively. As well as influencing whether children participate in sport at all, adults have an enormous impact on the types of sports in which they become involved, and whether that sport experience is negative or positive. In children's sport, it appears that a number of social influences often produce a clash of values between adult expectations of success and children's expectations of fun (Roberts et al., 1994). Consequently, 'parents' value systems and the role they play in structuring children's attitudes to sport, where children's well-being can become secondary, is most disturbing' (Kidman, 1998, p. 1). Because the desire for adult approval is very strong before puberty, children's ability to perform at their own level and for fun can be inhibited. Therefore adults have a responsibility to consider which expectations are their own and which are their children's. This is a difficult task because it requires some degree of objectivity.

To the extent that parents value and give attention to sports, children learn to see sports as worthwhile activities. The problem is that children's participation in sport is determined by adults who have designed competitions that reflect our adult expectations and are derived from our adult structures. Adults, including coaches, believe that they know what is best for children. We tend to dismiss or ignore the reality that while adult-structured competition can enable children to have a wonderful experience, for many children their experience of it can be totally unsuccessful and sometimes dreadful. Adult-structured competition has an enormous effect on children's self-esteem and their perceptions of their own ability.

General self-esteem, defined as one's evaluation of general self-worth, has been shown to play an important role in children's perception of and confidence in their ability to perform the task at hand, as well as influencing their social perception. Children low in self-esteem respond more positively to coaches who are trained to be reinforcing and supportive, and less positively to untrained coaches, than do children high in self-esteem (Smoll & Smith, 1989). Self-esteem is also related to how athletes perceive both positive and negative coach behaviours. Children with high levels of anxiety (which competition can create) are particularly sensitive when something threatens their self-esteem. For example, anxious children may perceive a coach as less reinforcing and encouraging and as more punitive than the coach actually is, because they are more likely to perceive behaviours as threatening. It is also possible that certain children are uncomfortable with high levels of reinforcement while, because of their life experiences, they expect and are relatively comfortable with negative interpersonal feedback. All life experiences, including sport, contribute to developing a balanced and healthy lifestyle and influence self-esteem.

The key ingredient to encouraging a high self-esteem is to ensure children have personal success, as when they feel that they have accomplished something, their confidence increases. All children need to have success so that they feel able to try new things and have fun with what they are doing. Inappropriate criticism can be a critical impediment to this learning. If they are constantly criticised for mistakes, children decide that learning is a dreaded thing. A child's low self-esteem comes from learning to expect failure when he or she does something.

Thus the 'win-at-all cost' attitude, which is largely associated with adult-structured competition and often comes from influential adults (such as parents and coaches), can significantly affect the way children perceive success. Winning promotes failure because 'winning' is often out of one's control and losing often equates to failure. Adult reinforcement is the main influence on the way children perceive failure. If adults make it clear that they expect their children to win, they insinuate that the children will fail unless they win. Constantly reinforcing this concept of winning perpetuates the adverse perception that if children do not win, they are not successful within their influential relationships. As a result, many children drop out of sport due to stress and their perception that they cannot be accepted.

As adults have such a major impact on young children, it is important for adults to use competition in ways that will teach sound values and attitudes. If competition meets children's needs for experience and life-long learning, it can be a positive tool. The following are some advantages to this kind of use of competition:

- Children can develop a positive self-image by participating in sport. If adults are encouraging and fair to all children and ensure that they are successful, children will value their involvement in sport and enhance their self-image.

- Children can learn the value of cooperation through sport. Indeed, learning to cooperate by being part of a team has been rationalised as a positive outcome of team sport participation for decades.

- Adults can reinforce the value of cooperation by ensuring that all children are treated fairly, by valuing the contributions of all team members, and by providing opportunities for all children to work together in practices and competitions.

- The powerful lessons that can be learned in such an environment may even be able to be transferred to other social situations such as family life and school.

- Children can develop social skills by participating in sport.

- One of the primary reasons that children participate is to meet new friends. Sport is simply one more avenue for children to develop friendships, and for many the friendships that are developed through sport become some of the strongest in their lives.

- If organised and conducted appropriately, sport participation can teach children fair play and sportsmanship.

- Unfortunately when winning is so important, children also learn how to cheat. Again, adults should teach fair play and respect by practising it themselves (Kidman & McKenzie, 1998, p. 11).

Competition is great if children see it to be successful. Success does not mean winning, but enjoying the experience and learning. Remember that because young children do not really understand competition, they will listen and act the way parents and other adults act. For this reason, adults need to be particularly careful not to put too many pressures on children, or they may not enjoy their sport and ultimately drop out.

Why Do Children Participate?

According to research, the main reasons why children participate in sport are to have fun, be with friends and improve skills (Taggart & Sharp, 1997). These reasons are forms of intrinsic or internal motivation, where high self-concept and feeling good are related to being satisfied with participation. With internal motivation, children tend to want to participate to satisfy themselves and want to improve for themselves. On the other hand, if children relate achievement to external rewards, they tend to want to participate to win or to impress someone else.

As mentioned above, significant adults are a primary influence on the degree to which children enjoy their sporting experience. As having fun is one of children's main reasons for participating in sport, whether they experience enjoyment is a major consideration in a decision over whether to continue participating. Behaviour of the individual parent, teacher, administrator or coach can affect children's enjoyment. More than that, it affects their psychosocial development (including attitudes, values and self-perception) beyond the influence of the school, curriculum, sport club or sport programme itself. The young athletes' perception of themselves as good, competent or otherwise in turn affects their reasons for participating.

Developing a competitive orientation

Sport psychologists have researched the influences on children's attitudes to participation in sport. Their focus is the concept of *competitive orientation* (Nicholls, 1989), which identifies some children as ego-oriented and others as mastery-oriented.

An *ego-oriented* child wants to look good for external reasons and compares himself or herself with others. Caring greatly about what others think, ego-oriented children are subject to pressures outside their control and the expectations of adults play a significant role. When under heavy pressure (as often applied by influential adults), they have a high ego orientation. Results of competition are important, as self-confidence is linked to performance. While ego-oriented children are winning, they are confident, but if they fail, they lose confidence and the desire to participate. For children with a high ego orientation, it is important to balance it with some degree of mastery focus.

A child who is *mastery-oriented* wants to become good at a sport for internal reasons. Such children want to determine how much they have improved. They will be satisfied with losing if they judge themselves to have performed well, or conversely dissatisfied with winning if they consider that they did not perform well.

Research is inconclusive about whether a child is born with a tendency to be ego- or mastery-oriented. It is believed that both tendencies can exist within each individual and that significant others can have a major influence in developing a particular orientation of a child (Murphy, 1999).

Social learning theory (Bandura, 1977) proposes that people learn new behaviours simply by observing and listening to others. Thus adults can influence children's cultural and social development. According to this theory, by observing parents and coaches on the sidelines, children learn to model their behaviours. These behaviours, in turn, can be perceived as appropriate or inappropriate according to cultural expectations and the existing values of parents and other adults.

These adult behaviours can also be categorised into mastery and/or ego-oriented tendencies. If an adult is ego-oriented, children who have observed and listened to that adult, will learn to be ego-oriented. Then if parents make negative comments (which have been deemed inappropriate in research findings), children often experience stress as they are publicly scrutinised and evaluated. With constant social evaluation, children have to be concerned with not only their ability to perform, but also how their parents behave during the competition. Consequently, if a child receives outcome-specific recognition, such as from a parent on the sideline (i.e. concerned with scoring, winning), then the child receives a clear message that the more important goals of achievement in sport are outcome-related. Conversely, if children receive recognition based on mastery (e.g. skill learning, performance) then they learn that the more important goals are mastery-oriented (Roberts & Treasure, 1995).

A child's need for adult and peer recognition highlights the influence of significant others on the environment and success in sport participation. The world of sport strongly reinforces an ego orientation because of the traditional expectations about 'winning'. Often the first question that parents ask children when they return home after a sporting event is, 'Did you win?', indicating that the adults see winning as the reward for sport and expect the children to fulfil the adult desire to win.

Research has also traced how children may develop towards a particular competitive orientation. Before approximately nine years of age, few children distinguish between ability and effort. In other words, most children cannot determine whether someone beat them (outcome, comparison to others) because of his or her greater talent (ability) or because he or she tried harder (effort). They may begin to see that some have more ability than others, but they still believe that effort will overcome ability. As discussed above, young children are highly influenced by and dependent on adult feedback (approval or disapproval), such that competition is really an adult-structured phenomenon that adults perceive as important but children do not really understand.

As children enter the 9–11-year-old category, they begin to see the difference between ability and effort. Their judgement moves from an external source (adults, peers) to an internal (self) source. By the age of 11, a perceived failure has a more significant impact on sporting self-confidence, because these children are likely to attribute it to a lack of ability. As this perceived lack of ability becomes significant to a child, this individual tends to leave sport because of the perception that he or she 'can't' do it well (Murphy, 1999). Based on this outcome of perceived lack of ability and the high drop-out rates that may result, it may be concluded that adult-structured competition and organised sport are not necessarily beneficial for children.

The benefits of a mastery orientation

For children to have long-term success, it is important for them to have a high mastery orientation, with adults encouraging and supporting mastery-type experiences for them in sport. A mastery climate encourages the child to apply effort, because it is associated with higher intrinsic motivation. Therefore significant others need to encourage the development of such motivation by emphasising process rather than outcome. In addition, sport psychology research has provided evidence that children tend to correlate fun and enjoyment with a mastery climate rather than with a climate focused on outcome (Cresswell, 1997).

A mastery orientation enables athletes to accept failure and to learn through trial and error. It focuses them on improving, rather than just on winning. To help develop this orientation, adults can encourage athletes to participate for their own goals and satisfaction (a goal in an empowerment approach), rather than for external reasons. Athletes need to learn how to judge their own progress, set their own goals and to take satisfaction from improving, even in defeat. The mastery approach enables athletes to think critically and independently, with both sport and life skills.

As the above discussion indicates, a mastery orientation is reflected clearly in the philosophy of empowerment as an approach to coaching. Although Wayne Smith, Hugh Galvan and Paul McKay do not speak of it specifically (Chapters Three and Four), they actively promote the idea of mastery orientation when they are concerned with learning for the benefit of the athletes themselves.

Encouraging a mastery orientation

Given that mastery-oriented children are more likely to participate and continue in sport, it is important for adults to know how to encourage mastery in children. As Wayne Smith has mentioned (Chapter Three; see also Chapter One), success and winning are different. For success, striving to win is more important than actually winning. A child can execute the best performance of his or her life and still lose the competition. This child can still feel positive because, when success is determined by the individual child as it is among mastery-oriented children, success is equal to good performance and meeting self-determined goals. Every little success deserves to be rewarded through encouragement and support.

As Murphy (1999) suggested, in teaching young athletes mastery orientation, adults need to:

- Encourage realistic goal-setting,
- When finding a coach, look for,
    - Valuing qualities beyond winning (love of the game),
    - Knowledge of the sport,
    - Ability to encourage,
    - A love of teaching,
- Emphasise progress, not outcome,
- Emphasise participation for all,
- Reward skill development,
- Encourage self-awareness (problem solving).

All these qualities are closely linked to an empowerment philosophy.

Why Do Children Drop Out?

The discussion so far has indicated that children's sporting experiences can influence their individual development in both positive and negative directions. Research has suggested that a significant number of children drop out of sport because of their negative experiences of it. As adults, we are sometimes responsible for these negative experiences. Although we tend to know that children should be encouraged, our emotions, love of winning and pursuit of what we think is best for our children can override our intention to provide a positive environment.

Many studies have examined why children participate in sport, but few have focused on dropping out. Among the few studies conducted in this area, the reasons for dropping out tend to be that the children had other interests, the coach was too tough/mean, it was no longer fun or they did not get enough chance to participate (Gould & Petlichkoff, 1988). Interestingly, as reinforced by Hugh Galvan and Paul McKay (see Chapter Four), children seldom say that their desire 'to win' (a characteristic goal of a tough/mean coach) is a reason for participating.

Although many coaches and other adults have tried to reduce the high drop-out rate in various sports, many still promote winning as all-important and put unnecessary pressure on children. These attitudes are encouraged by society more widely, which values winning and the competitive achievements of élite athletes. It is also obvious to all adults that society puts most of our sport-directed monies into 'élite' sport. It is what society values most. Yet this view overlooks the reality that there would be no élite sport unless children are developed and want to participate and stay in sport.

Contributing to such pressures is the value that professional sport attaches to certain kinds of performance. Professional sport emphasises winning, entertainment, money and, in certain sports, aggression. Despite children's limited skill, knowledge and understanding of tactics and strategies, many adults expect children to participate and act like professionals, when the children simply want to have fun and to be with their friends.

Certainly, there are many coaches who focus on attracting and keeping children involved by providing a positive, safe and supportive environment that caters for children's needs in sport. Not surprisingly, such a supportive environment is related to an empowering style of coaching. If adults can ensure that such positive environments can be provided for children, then fewer children will drop out. Unfortunately, these environments are not always established.

As indicated above, one of the main reasons that children drop out of sport is that for them it is no longer fun. In many instances, adults intend to encourage children to focus on having fun, being with friends and developing skills but, as the competition gets underway, some parents (a minority) become increasingly excited and concerned about the performance of their son or daughter, and the outcome of the competition. This emotion is also true of many coaches.

In clubs, the sport itself is geared towards competition, including for children. For example, there are sports where league standings are kept for under 10s and some sports even have national competitions for children under 10 years (despite the research suggesting that children under 11 do not really understand the notion of competition). This kind of environment is the perfect set-up for children to experience excessive stress and anxiety and maybe, as a result, drop out of the sport. If the emphasis is truly on having fun, being with friends and skill development, then why is there a need for league standings and competition points?

A focus on winning can have a secondary effect on coaching that also discourages children from continuing with sport. As suggested in Hugh and Paul's player evaluations (see Chapter Four) and reinforced by research findings, athletes *do* want to participate rather than sit on the sideline. It is important to find out the coach's philosophy and whether he or she intends to allow equal time for all. As part of the empowerment philosophy, all children should receive the opportunity to participate equally, as reflected in the various rotation systems of empowering coaches (see Chapters Three and Four).

Parents have a range of expectations for their children in sport. Some wish their children to do well because they themselves missed out on opportunities in childhood, or live vicariously through their children, hoping to gain glory and satisfaction from their children's success (Brower, 1979). Worries about failure and living up to adult expectations and social evaluation add unneeded stress to children and can lead them to drop out. Adults who are themselves involved in competitive sport tend to increase their children's anxiety and the chances of burnout because of the complex interplay of their values and the personal characteristics inherent in the child (Gould, 1993).

One of the mismatches in youth sport is that most children are actually mastery-oriented and parents reinforce winning, which falls into the realm of ego orientation (Cresswell, 1997). This conflict of interest increases the likelihood that children will drop out. Children still suggest that winning is important to them, but it is less important than having fun, being with friends and improving skills (again, see Hugh and Paul's player evaluations in Chapter Four). Given that winning is generally out of the control of athletes (due to uncontrollable factors like opposition and referee calls), the most effective method of decreasing the drop-out rate appears to be focusing on the reasons that children play sport.

Adults on the Sideline

Children who perceive themselves as low in competence are particularly dependent on, or are easily affected by, external feedback (Horn & Hasbrook, 1987). Consequently, their experience of negative comments from their parents may be detrimental. On the other hand, if significant adults evaluate their performance attempts in terms of mastery and give them encouraging and contingent feedback, children are likely to perceive that they performed with some degree of success. They tend to develop a positive perception of their competence and a belief that they can control future performance outcomes (Horn & Hasbrook, 1987).

The sideline behaviour of adults is most noticeable to young children. For example, a gentleman on the sideline at a soccer game of under-seven-year-olds yelled out to the children, 'Come on you guys, pull up your socks'. As a result, the game stopped and all of the players pulled up their socks! This true-life example shows how much such sideline comments and behaviours influence children who are participating:

> Children do hear and listen to what their parents and other adults are saying on the sideline. Most children don't say anything, but the negative or embarrassing feelings that they experience are real. When children are asked about what they want adults to say, they mostly suggest 'just cheering'! (Kidman & McKenzie, 1998, p. 20)

One of the common intentions of adults on the sideline is to ensure that their children do their best and do what they are supposed to do. They may shout out corrections or instructions from the sideline, assuming they are helping. Unfortunately, their good intentions can backfire as these adults are being prescriptive in their behaviour, not empowering. As stated in previous chapters, for children to learn, they should make decisions in a variety of situations. When adults on the sideline relay instructions to children in competition, the children simply follow those instructions. The children lose the opportunity to practise decision-making, and thus lose the opportunity for maximal learning (Hellison, 1985).

With the recognition that decision-making is an important skill to develop, an empowering approach gains more credence for its encouragement of decision making in athletes. If children are given opportunities to interpret information that is available to them while they are performing, and to decide for themselves the appropriate course of action, they will learn more and retain more information. They may not make the decision that an observing adult expects, but in making it the young athletes will have learned something about their performance as they are being encouraged to be self-aware. It is also amazing what children can teach adults when they are left to make unique decisions.

As some research has suggested, most comments from adults on the sideline are quite positive, but a significant proportion (about one-third) may be described as negative (Kidman, McKenzie & McKenzie, 1999). This proportion is far too high to create a positive sporting experience for children. Adults need to be made aware that negative comments from the sideline can put unnecessary pressure on the children who they are watching and supporting. It is important not to yell at them for making a mistake in front of their friends and other spectators, as it can decrease their self-confidence, increasing the likelihood of those children dropping out of the sport.

In a survey of hockey players under 12 years of age, Suzie Pearce (1996) examined the influences and comments of adults on the sideline. She found that although children generally like to have adults there for support, this need was not met: 50 per cent of parents came to watch their children play, but 95 per cent of the children reported that they would like their parents to come. Of those who did not want their parents to come, some said that they were embarrassed when their parents did come because of what their parents said on the sideline and because they did not want to fail in front of their parents. These results suggest that some adults who come to watch may put too much pressure on their children.

A good way to determine whether the sideline comments are helpful and supportive is to ask the children what they prefer to hear on the sideline, if anything. Some children do not hear what goes on. However, many children hear exactly what the expectations of adults are. It is important to listen to what children prefer to hear on the sideline and then try to put it into practice. Also, to support children, adults need to eliminate the question, 'Did you win?' when they come home from the game. This question sends a clear message that winning is what is important. Children often have goals they are working towards. Try asking them if and how they met their goals, or 'How was the game today?' The types of questions that adults ask their children can convey a particular message.

In summary, adults (especially parents) need to reduce the level of negative and outcome-related comments in public (e.g. from the sideline) and in private (e.g. after the game). Instead, they need to encourage children's notion of success in sport (i.e. to have fun, meet new friends and improve skills) and enhance children's self-esteem by focusing on a process in sport rather than on the outcome of sport.

Useful guidelines for adults on the sidelines

- Yell encouraging comments and keep the voice tone positive.
- Let the coach do his/her job. Like the children, they are doing their best.
- Stay in the area designated for spectators.
- Understand that the referees/umpires are doing the best they can. Have faith in them and thank them for officiating at the end of the game or event.
- Offer to help the coach, referee or scorers.
- Show self-control. Remember, you are watching children participate in sport—it is not the Olympic Games.
- Cheer for the entire team and encourage all players.
- Provide support for your child by listening to them and trying to understand their feelings.
- Be a good role model. Avoid smoking and drinking at children's sporting events.

Congratulate the opposing players/athletes at the end of the event (Kidman & McKenzie, 1998, p. 22)

Sport as Only One Part of a Child's Life

When adults get caught up in the emotions and challenges of sport, often, subconsciously, they encourage their children to neglect other important adventures in life. Children have homework, other interests, a family and friends. Sometimes sport can take over a young one's life because adults are 'overinvolved'. Adults, including parents and coaches, should reflect on their own priorities and try to ensure that their child achieves a balance by showing interest in other parts of their child's life. As Craig Lewis mentions in Chapter Seven, children need to be allowed to balance their commitments, with sport as only a part of their young life.

As well as occupying a central position in the athletic setting, a coach can have an influence that extends into other areas of a child's life. Ultimately, a coach's effect on the athletes is determined by the meaning that athletes attach to his or her behaviours. In other words, the young athletes' processes of thinking and emotional well-being filter the obvious coaching behaviours, in their development of attitudes toward their coach and sporting experience. We would expect that athletes' notions of how coaches are expected to behave would influence how they react to particular behaviours. For example, punitive behaviours may be expected and tolerated to a greater degree in a collision sport like football.

The adults who work with youth sport programmes would be wise to use what they know about children's informal sports to guide their attempts to organise those programmes to meet the needs of young people. If children enjoy what they experience in organised sport, they are more likely to be favourably influenced by the relationships they form through their participation.

Conclusion

Many highly competitive adults tend to 'exploit' children based on their own needs and values. It is not a question of blame: most adults are trying to what is best for their children, but sometimes they get it wrong. The solution is to give priority to the development needs of children, ahead of adult needs. Murphy (1999) suggested that in the context of competitive sports, coaches and other adults can achieved this focus by enabling their athletes to:

· learn emotional and psychological skills to help them become effective competitors and give them life-long skills;

·   learn how to deal with loss, without transferring or reinforcing blame on children;

·   focus on achieving a mastery orientation in their approach to improving children's performance; and

·   learn new skills, work on existing skills, to set goals and try to achieve them and to work with others in forming a positive team culture.

All these skills are useful in everyday life as well as sport. As such, they allow all athletes to benefit from sport.

Teachers, coaches and parents have such a major impact on the quality of children's sporting experiences that we need to reflect on the opportunities we can provide for them. Our influence can help ensure a positive experience and a sound level of development. If children are happy and successful, under little or no pressure to win, they enjoy their experience in sport.

Children learn what they live. Therefore they should be taught and encouraged in a positive learning environment. Children and adults can share in the enjoyment of sport for a multitude of reasons. Enjoy your short time with your children. Help them to grow through sport. Help them to create fond sporting memories that you can both enjoy for a long time.

The first duty to children is to make them happy. If you have not made them so, you have wronged them. No other good they may get can make up for that.

—Charles Buxton, English author

References

Bandura, A. (1977). *Social Learning Theory.* Englewood Cliffs, NJ: Prentice-Hall.

Brower, J.J. (1979). The professionalization of organized youth sport: social psychological impacts and outcomes, *Annals of the American Academy of Political and Social Science, 445,* 39–46.

Coakley, J. (1992). Burnout among adolescent athletes: a personal failure or social problem? *Sociology of Sport Journal, 9*(3), 271–285.

Cresswell, S. (1997). *Intrinsic Motivation in Youth Sport: The Effect of Goal Orientations and Motivational Climate.* An unpublished dissertation: University of Otago.

Gould, D. (1993). Intensive sport participation and the prepubescent athletes: competitive stress and burnout. In B.R. Cahill & A.J. Pearl (eds), *Intensive Participation in Children's Sport* (pp. 19–38). Champaign, IL: Human Kinetics.

Gould, D., & Petlichkoff, L. (1988). Psychological stress and the age-group wrestler. In E.W. Brown & C.F. Banta (eds), *Competitive Sports for Children and Youth* (pp. 63–73). Champaign, IL: Human Kinetics.

Hellison, D. (1985). *Goals and Strategies for Teaching Physical Education.* Champaign, IL: Human Kinetics.

Horn, T., & Hasbrook, C.A. (1987). Psychological characteristics and the criteria children use for self-evaluation, *Journal of Sport Psychology, 9,* 208–221.

Kidman, L. (1998). Who reaps the benefits in coaching research? The case for an applied sociological approach, *Sociology of Sport On Line, 1*(2), article 1.

Kidman, L. & McKenzie, A. (1998). *Your Kids, Their Game: A Children's Guide for Parents and Caregivers in Sport.* Australian Sports Commission, Active Australia.

Kidman, L., McKenzie, A., & McKenzie, B. (1999). The nature and target of parents' comments during youth sport competitions, *Journal of Sport Behavior, 22*(1), 54–68.

Murphy, S. (1999). *The Cheers and the Tears: A Healthy Alternative to the Dark Side of Youth Sports Today.* San Francisco, CA: Jossey-Bass.

Nicholls, J. (1989). *The Competitive Ethos and Democratic Education,* Cambridge, Mass: Harvard University.

Pearce, S. N. (1996). *Pre-adolescent Hockey Players' Perceptions of Parental Behaviours.* An unpublished dissertation, University of Otago.

Roberts, G.C., Treasure, D.C., & Hall, H.K. (1994). Parental goal orientations and beliefs about the competitive-sport experience of their child, *Journal of Applied Social Psychology, 24,* 631–645.

Roberts, G.C., & Treasure, D.C. (1995). Achievement goals, motivational climate and achievement strategies and behaviors in sport, *International Journal of Sport Psychology, 26,* 64–80.

Smoll, F.L., & Smith, R.E. (1989). Leadership behaviors in sport: a theoretical model and research paradigm. *Journal of Applied Social Psychology, 19*(18), 1522–1551.

Taggart, A., & Sharp, S. (1997). *Adolescents and Sport: Determinants of Current and Future Participation.* Perth: Sport and Physical Activity Research Centre, Edith Cowan University.

Each day of our lives we make deposits in the memory banks of our children.

—*Charles Swindoll*

Chapter Ten

Take the attitude of a student. Never be too big to ask questions, never know too much to learn something new.

—Og Mandino

So, What Now?

Developing Decision Makers has highlighted empowerment as a motivational approach that coaches can use to provide a more innovative sport environment for empowered athletes. Now that you have been 'convinced' that this is a great approach worth trying, it is important for you to know how you might begin. Throughout this book, contributors have illustrated the benefits and challenges of empowerment from their own successful experience. All have suggested ways to trial the approach. So use their experience to get out there and start.

This chapter discusses initial implementation (giving it a go), then how you might evaluate your empowerment and how you can continue to develop as a coach. It is important to note that the way you coach now is probably terrific and has great merit. Empowerment is a way to enhance your coaching and enhance athletes' performance. As Rod Thorpe points out in Chapter Two, there is no right way to coach, but there are several better ways to coach:

> You will choose coaching methods to suit your persona. This said, just as a good player does not try only one method of beating an opponent, so a coach should develop a range of approaches. Consider adding this to your coaching portfolio and then decide if it works better for you. I am convinced that the traditional way has shortfalls, but I am quite willing to accept that many coaches will employ it at some points as part of a variety of approaches. Once you do this and see the 'power' of 'empowering', you may start to develop a philosophy which is much more about developing the player as a whole, and I do mean as a person as well as a sports performer.

Putting it into Practice

First, let's summarise what the various contributors have said. Each and every one of them has suggested that it is important to at least 'give empowerment a go'. You will probably not feel accomplished the first time you try it but, as you develop it, empowerment becomes a powerful way to enable athletes to learn, be motivated to put in huge effort and to enjoy their sporting experience. As a result, their performance will naturally improve. As Rod Thorpe, Wayne Smith, Hugh Gavan, Paul McKay and Robyn Jones have all noted, if you have never tried this approach, you need to implement it in small steps. Rod sums up this strategy well:

Rod: Start small. You will have well tried coaching model in your head from your previous experience as a coach and very powerfully from the way you were coached. See if you cannot introduce elements into your sessions in which you give more freedom to players … We have all done it, but what we usually do is select the activity that allows us, the coach, to 'tell' the players what we want them to do. The major difference is that we help them work out what they have to do to exploit the situation and this means 'questioning' either verbally or by setting a new condition in the game.

One of the real hurdles to overcome is having the confidence to try empowerment. It is important to accept that you may not be successful the first time; remember that a big step towards success in your use of the approach is just getting in and learning it, applying it and seeing how the athletes respond. As Paul suggests:

Paul: Don't be afraid to experiment because how do you know how it works, until you put it into action? You can get all the information you like but if you don't practise it, you are not going to get the confidence to use it and you're not going to know how the players react. If you are doing research, the whole self-reflection comes into it. There are so many aspects to it. It is a lot of learning. That is why it is so daunting because there is all this new information to process. I am still daunted by it now (after a year of doing it). Perseverance is the key.

The empowerment approach does not succeed on its own. It is important for you as coach to continually develop and practise your empowering strategies (just as in any skill learning). Your athletes (if they have never been coached in this way) must also 'buy in' to the approach before it can be successful. Gaining the support of some athletes may take time, along with effort in facilitating and nurturing. Wayne reinforces this idea with reference to his own development of the approach with the Canterbury Crusaders:

Wayne: It is going to take a while … and that's what people don't understand. If the quality outcome you are after is satisfaction, then we got that straight away. As I said the first year was exciting. Since then, we have won the tournament twice, but to me it's not the winning that counts—it's doing your best to win. Having fun and learning together is a rewarding experience. We've had hard times, but generally the smile on their faces is the biggest indicator to success. Seeing a group of talented individuals selflessly giving to each other and enjoying the experience makes coaching worthwhile.

Because athletes may not all catch on to the whole approach together, coaches must cater for individual needs and nurture each athlete. In a sense, the coach has to continue to 'sell' the approach and enable athletes to understand the benefits they may gain through it. Robyn has noted:

Robyn: To overcome such challenges, a coach must tread warily and considerately, initially making sure that the athletes understand the ultimate goals of the philosophy, and also that they are sincerely buying in to the new strategy. In this way, the coach ensures that the athletes realise how the new approach can help them reach their goals. To introduce empowerment, the coach should carefully and realistically explain its aims and methods before launching into a series of questions. The aim of such questions should be not only to identify the motivations and goals of the children, but also to check their understanding of the objective of the exercises and how both the approach and the drills benefit their sporting development.

One of the most challenging, yet rewarding aspects of this coaching strategy is the need to draw on the 'art' of coaching. This art includes the ability to read and understand your athletes, then help them by using great communication and coaching strategies that are suitable for the athlete in that particular situation. Robyn has elaborated on what it means for a coach to successfully apply the art of coaching through an empowerment approach:

Robyn: Perhaps the hardest part of implementing a theory of empowerment at any level is having the patience to let it run at the speed of the athletes (Arai, 1997). This pace, as Arai (1997) notes, is often much slower than a coach imagines. The athletes must first become open to change, which expresses itself in a need and desire for it, and a recognition of its value. Remaining patient is not always easy for coaches, who traditionally like, and often need, short-term gratification and results from their work. If coaches try to force this change, however, they are likely to hinder athletes' acceptance of the philosophy and instead create resistance to its adoption. Therefore a prerequisite of successful implementation is to patiently support and encourage the athletes to accept and integrate the empowerment philosophy at their own speed. To achieve a shared ownership of common goals, a coach must respect the individuality of each athlete.

Determining when to jump in and when to leave the athletes to make their own decisions is another important facet to the art of coaching. Judging the situation correctly takes time while the coach tries it out in different contexts, and it is not uncommon to make mistakes along the way. We learn best through trial and error.

As Wayne points out, one of the most 'different' aspects of the empowering approach is that the coach stands back and observes for longer, enabling the athletes to make decisions. If we, as coaches, jump in and try to 'take over', little learning occurs. So, when observing and analysing your athletes, you might try counting 5 to 10 seconds, or allowing several trials of the game, before providing feedback. Then when providing feedback, jump in with a meaningful, open-ended question that enables athletes to think and become self-aware (see Chapter Eight).

Clearly then, when the coach does jump in, it is important to ask the right question. As Wayne, Robyn and Rod point out, it can be tempting to tell people what you know. A lot of coaches who have never tried an empowerment approach feel that they must tell their athletes everything they know. Even when attempting to pose a question, they often answer it for the athletes. With reference to the ideas from this book, what outcomes are likely from this kind of coaching approach? How do athletes feel when their knowledge is undermined? Questioning is not easy, but it is thoroughly worthwhile when athletes make informed decisions because of what they learn. Therefore, planning and practising are critical. Paul comments on his process of learning how to question as a junior coach:

> **Paul:** Questioning is a really difficult thing to do. You actually have to know a lot of answers and you've got to know how to aim your questioning to get the answer. That is where the manipulation comes in. You've got the answer, but you try to manipulate your questions so that they come up with the answers (probing). You have to be really careful not to give them the answer because it is very tempting to do. If you ask a question, 'How are you going to get past those defenders?' and they don't come up with your answers, it is sometimes very easy to just give them the answer.

As coaches, we continually look for better ways to enhance the performance of our athletes. Our search is a process of learning and practising that will give us that 'edge'. As Robyn suggests:

> **Robyn:** It is important to remember that empowerment is never truly complete, as new challenges continually rise; these challenges are often linked to the uniqueness of each athlete, the interaction between athletes and the particular context of each interaction.

So allow athletes to interact and question. It will enhance your coaching approach even further, once they understand it, value it and become more self-aware and better decision-makers.

In summary, the following are some key points for putting an empowerment approach into practice:

· Go for it. Empowerment is a fantastic approach, enhancing learning and the sport environment.

· Take small steps. You cannot be proficient immediately, it takes practice.

· Tell your athletes about the approach, so they can begin to understand why you are using it.

· Add the approach to your current practice as another part of your coaching repertoire.

· Cater for athletes, remember patience is a virtue.

· Observe your athletes for a period before jumping in. Often athletes are already self-aware and can fix errors on their own.

· Ask meaningful questions, but remember this takes time, so practise them.

· Evaluate:

  – how your approach is working;

  – how athletes are responding to it; and

  – your questioning repertoire.

· Be careful not to overquestion and not to answer your own questions.

· Most of all, enjoy using the empowerment approach—your athletes sure will.

Self-reflection—A Key to Developing and Improving Your Coaching

An important part of learning any approach, including empowerment, is to self-reflect on your own coaching. Self-reflection is a particularly significant part of empowerment, whereby coaches themselves take ownership of their own learning and decision making. Each coach should take responsibility to evaluate the way he or she coaches, the way the athletes respond and the general team environment.

Just as coaches expect athletes to practise to improve their performance (physical, mental and social), coaches need to practise their coaching performance. Extending this analogy, we would expect that if coaches do not evaluate what they do, it is difficult for them to achieve a high standard of performance. A successful, empowering coach should practise and understand the theoretical elements of sport and coaching as well as technical fundamentals of instruction. From their own experience, Wayne, Hugh and Paul suggest that self-analysis is a way to continue improving and learning about coaching at both élite and junior levels:

Wayne: When I first committed to using empowerment in my coaching, there was no one else really using it, so I needed to look at other sports to keep learning. I still like to see what other coaches do and whether I am on the right track or not. I know the way I want to go … to continue empowering my players and to get better at questioning.

I have to work on my ability to discriminate between the need to ask questions about the skill and the need to ask about the tactics, e.g. understand whether it's a skill issue that let the player down or whether he didn't understand the game. Did he fail to pass because he couldn't technically execute it quickly enough, or did he pass because he couldn't see what was [going] on? You can get the answer quickly ... by asking, 'What did you do?', 'What did you see?' and 'What did you want to do?' You can soon find out whether he wanted to pass and couldn't or whether he ran with it because he didn't see that the pass was on.

The skill is in understanding how to use the questions and doing it quickly and selectively so that you're observing more than talking. Let the players have a go, then if you see the activity being done correctly you don't need to step in. My biggest fault is overquestioning.

Hugh: Reading books and articles, discussions with other people and watching other coaches question their players, videoing yourself coaching and reflecting on your performance, are great ways to assess your questioning skills ... you learn a lot about your ability to develop meaningful questions from the players' answers. A blank look on a player's face lets you know your questions need work. I think that I'd always used questioning in some form, but certainly not with the same understanding that I think I now have.

Paul: You've really got to take the whole element of the self-reflection, reading your athletes, developing your ability to see their reactions. The way that they react, you will know straight away whether it has worked or if it hasn't worked. [It is important to be] able to put your ego aside and say to someone else, 'Please give me a hand. What have I done well and what do I need to improve on?'

A lot of people can't take a bit of criticism. It doesn't have to be negative, it could be constructive: 'Instead of doing this, why don't you try this one next time?' You have to be open to ideas from other people. It doesn't have to be coaches, it could be one of your friends on the sideline. So the athletes, other people's feedback, and research, all together are all great ways to learn about coaching and yes, we will always be learning (as Rod Thorpe said).

Self-reflection empowers coaches to accept the challenge to become the best coaches they can be. Videotaping, a useful tool for a self-reflective process in teacher education, has gained great status in coach education as a means to self-train, as Wayne describes:

Wayne: ... we film our trainings to look at the drills we are doing and make sure they are valid, see whether the players are doing them really well and to check our way of communicating. Quite often I go home and think, 'Gee that wasn't the right way to handle that player tonight'. I've had to learn strategies to cope with people making mistakes. I have very competitive instincts and like to see everything done well. It has been an ongoing learning experience allowing the players to make errors along the way.

Many coaches have already used videotapes of their trainings, as an

insightful means of observing their own coaching. For those who have never tried, it is a daunting task at first, as many people, when confronting themselves on videotape, are surprised at their physical image. This confrontation is a barrier that you have to overcome, by getting accustomed to and accepting mannerisms that only you notice. Thereafter you can objectively and realistically look at your coaching, how your athletes are empowered, and what impact your philosophy and methods are having.

Figure 1 illustrates a model of how self-reflection works, whether or not you are using a videotape of your coaching to assist you in the process.

Figure 1: The Coaching Process — A Five-step Model for Self-reflection

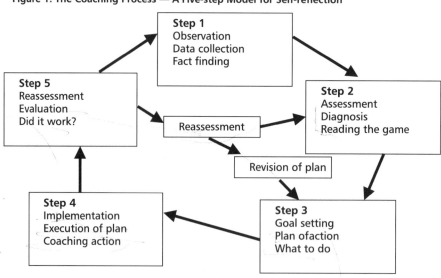

Source: Fairs, J.R. (1987). The coaching process: essence of coaching, *Sports Coach, 11*(1), p. 19. Copyright 1987 by Australian Coaching Council. Reprinted with permission.

The five-step model is designed for coaches to self-reflect by analysing, evaluating and modifying their coaching skills. In self-reflecting on what they do, coaches observe certain elements of the training session in a process of:

- collecting pertinent information;
- analysing the information;
- using the information to formulate goals and directions;
- designing a plan of action;

- implementing the plan of action;

- reassessing the outcome of the plan; and

- continually repeating the cycle.

The cycle continues for every aspect of coaching that a coach may wish to improve.

As highlighted consistently in this book, to enhance an empowering approach, coaches frequently use questioning and problem solving as tools to develop their athletes. Coaches should also ask themselves reflective questions as an important element of their ongoing self-analysis. Reflective questions provide guidelines and information about your coaching. They can also be designed to suit your own development needs. You may find it useful to ask sport-specific personnel or another respected person to help develop reflective questions about a particular strategy that you wish to analyse or change. This person would also be a good source for advice about your coaching (provided he or she has nothing to do with your coaching career, as that person's objectivity may be lost, while you may find your coaching becomes unrealistic and unnatural).

Sample questions: a starting point for self-analysis

Below are some examples of very general reflective questions about coaching. Although not specific to individual needs, they may be a starting point for your self-analysis (using your videotape to answer each question):

1. What did you learn about your coaching? and about your management?

2. What did you learn about the athletes?

3. What did athletes learn about themselves?

4. What effects did your coaching have on the athletes? Discuss benefits and barriers.

5. How can the athletes rectify any barriers discussed? How can you rectify any barriers discussed?

6. How do you think the session could be improved?

7. Do you think you can solve any identified coaching difficulties by yourself?

8. How do you plan to follow up in the next sessions?

9. How was this session relevant or transferable to other aspects of the athletes' lives?

10. What did you learn about yourself?

11. Describe in detail one significant event that happened during your lesson. It may be significant because it was something that excited you, bothered you, made you rethink your intentions/beliefs, or made you realise that your intentions/beliefs were sound.

Sample questions: a starting point for reflecting on your empowerment approach

The next set of general reflective questions may help to get you started in looking at how you use empowerment (again, referring to the videotape from the training session!):

1. How was the session designed to empower athletes? Analyse your planned questions.

2. Did athletes have input to training? How or why not?

3. Reflect on your session by answering these questions:

    (a) What did you like best about the session?

    (b) What did you like least about the session?

    (c) How would you improve the session plan?

    (d) What did the athlete(s) learn?

4. Analyse your line of questioning. Did it encourage athletes' learning? Were the questions clear? Were you flexible in your ability to ask purposeful questions?

5. Explain the general motivational climate of the session.

6. How well did you plan for different ability levels?

7. How well did you cater to athlete-centred learning? Explain.

8. How did athletes respond to being empowered? Give examples.

9. Explain how this training session nurtured the holistic needs of the athletes.

10. Are athletes' needs identified and how do you encourage independent development?

Sample questions: a starting point for reflecting on your use of Game Sense

As Chapter Two discusses, many empowering coaches make use of

Teaching Games for Understanding (Game Sense). The following reflective questions may help you to analyse how you use Game Sense in your training session:

1. Discuss how this session was designed to cater for Game Sense.

2. Analyse the games you provided. How can they be improved?

3. Analyse the purposefulness of the games.

4. How did athletes respond to the Game Sense session?

5. Did the athletes learn anything beneficial to their development? Why or why not?

6. Explain the social benefits and/or challenges of applying Game Sense in this lesson.

7. Analyse the enjoyment and motivation of the athletes participating in this session.

8. Were you happy with the amount of time that the athletes were able to practise for the session? Why or why not?

9. Analyse the questions you asked. Were they predominantly high-order or low-order questions?

10. How do you think the training session could be improved?

Sample questions: a starting point for reflecting on your questioning

Chapter Eight focuses on asking meaningful questions. Here are some questions for you that will help you reflect on your questioning of your athletes (using your video!):

1. How clear and coherent were the questions that you asked your athletes?

2. When asking questions, did you have the attention of all the athletes?

3. Analyse the responses to the questions. Who answered them? Did they give the answers that you expected? How well did you probe?

4. How well did you listen and accept athlete responses?

5. Did learning occur? Explain your answer.

6. List the questions that you asked during the session. How many were high-order questions and how many were low-order questions? Was the ratio effective? Why or why not?

7. Discuss any thinking that occurred (or did not occur) after you

asked high-order questions.

8. Were the questions meaningful to the purpose of the training session? Explain.

9. Were you flexible in accepting and exploring athletes' responses?

10. How well did you encourage your athletes to reflect and process what they learned? Explain.

To enhance your use of videotapes to analyse coaching, show the videotape to a colleague, coach, teacher or any person and ask for feedback. It is an advantage if this person comes from a similar philosophical belief so that he or she can help to analyse how you are using a particular empowering approach. The feedback enhances your learning, verifying what areas you need to develop, and is ultimately beneficial to the athletes. Your colleagues will also gain a lot from observing and analysing you; in this way, the learning process spreads throughout the coaching world.

Finally, coaches should obtain positive feedback both from other people and from themselves. Identify your positive strategies and 'pat yourself on the back' as much as you try to improve yourself.

Continuing Coach Development

As presented above, self-reflective analysis is a means of learning about and improving empowerment in coaching. An advantage of using videotaping as a tool in this process is that it is easy to apply. It does take time to sit down and analyse these videotapes, but once coaches become accustomed to using videotapes, they can participate in a self-directed training approach when it suits to their own needs and time.

An example of self-reflective analysis

The following outline of a self-reflective analysis process can aid in reviewing your coaching and targeting parts of your coaching you might want to improve.

Step 1:   Videotape a training session and conduct a self-reflective analysis of your coaching. Identify one or two parts of your coaching you want to change or improve. Give the videotape to a critical friend and gather feedback about your coaching. Tell the friend your philosophy and what you are intending to focus on. It is important that this critical friend acts as a sounding board rather than an adviser. You need to feel empowered with the process, meaning that it is you who decides what to change, for your reasons.

Step 2:   Develop a plan of action for changing or improving the parts you have identified. Ask yourself, 'How can I design a method to change/improve this part of my coaching?' You can get relevant reflective questions from a critical friend, another respected individual, or written resources (like this book or others that are in the library).

Step 3:   You will need several training sessions to work on improving each of the parts you identified. Use the first few training sessions to practise these parts. After practising, videotape another training session. Ensure you have prepared some reflective questions to help in the self-reflective analysis of this videotape.

Step 4:   Repeat the above process to focus on other parts of your coaching or to revisit parts you may have identified in the first process. Remember you can only work on one or two matters at a time, and it takes a long time master or get where you want it to be with some strategies.

Self-reflective analysis is one method that will help you to continue developing as a coach. Another way to continue developing as a coach (as Wayne, Hugh and Paul have suggested) is to do research. Research does not mean having to understand academic language and gobbledegook. What it does mean is read books, search the Internet, network with coaches, observe other coaches who use empowerment and attend conferences. Asking athletes can also help in your research.

Gathering information and continuing to learn

In some countries and some sport cultures, people do not communicate with the 'enemy' for fear of giving away secrets about team strategies. This attitude seems absurd, given that one of the main reasons we coach (at least from an empowering perspective) is to develop athletes. To develop philosophical beliefs, we need to talk with other people, including coaches, parents, administrators, athletes and educators.

By talking with other people who have insights from their own experience of what has and has not worked, we may gather ideas that may help individuals and teams. Perhaps you have a specific problem in designing a game that enhances an old drill that was used in a sport, so ask another coach for advice. You are not admitting defeat; you are demonstrating a desire to search for knowledge or new methods and to help athletes learn. It cannot hurt to ask. The worst that can happen is for someone to say, 'No'. Wayne, Hugh and Paul have indicated that they are always looking for advice to improve their coaching. They all say they have so much to learn, as coaches, that they continually search for better ways. Other coaches, parents and administrators have some great ideas. Ask anyone, everyone has an opinion, especially in sport.

Most athletes may have experienced several different coaches. Ask them for their opinion—and in the process apply a key element of the empowerment approach. Hugh and Paul have found that gaining a written evaluation from their players is extremely useful to their coaching development. The player evaluations pointed out positives and negatives of the season, information the coaches can use to 'better' their coaching for the next season. Through empowerment, coaches are constantly asking for player feedback, reading them and interpreting their ideas and values. Through empowerment, you can make a natural evaluation from the players when they answer questions and you 'read' them, which is useful to everything that occurs in the sporting environment.

Educators (teachers, university lecturers, coach educators) can offer great advice and information. Although some coaches may see educators as 'too academic' or out of their league, there are many educators who understand coaching as they have been there. Educators are able to benefit from keeping up to date with current research and many put these new strategies into practice. This perspective is where empowerment came from: coaches who have achieved great success, but realised that through an empowerment approach they can enable greater success and fulfilment among their athletes. Coaches should be empowered to enhance their coaching by having the 'nous' to search for better approaches.

Some speak of a 'gap' between educators and coaches but, in reality, many of us are trying to get rid of this perceived gap. Educators and coaches learn from each other; educators and coaches, as Paul has suggested, learn from athletes (and students). The athletes are the ones to benefit from this 'sharing of ideas'. Through this sharing, coaches can provide terrific learning experiences that enhance athletes' lifestyles, in which sport is a means to an end, rather than the end. No one has all the answers, but through conversations and observations we can learn from each other. Among the coaches interviewed for this book, a common characteristic is their belief that they are still learning. Their ego does not get in the way; rather, the athletes are truly more important than the sport.

Conclusion

It has been an intention of this book to inform and teach coaches about empowerment, including how athletes learn and enjoy their sport. Just as one goal of the book is to teach about empowerment, another goal is to empower coaches to increase their knowledge, practise more, reflect and analyse, and continue to improve in their own time and using their own methods. Coaches should provide athletes with choice and control; this book provides coaches with choice and control. Take bits from it that you think will work, and skip the bits that you have trouble with. The previous chapters have illustrated some successes, but this book does not have all the answers. It is an attempt to share ideas so that coaches can take the ones that suit their philosophy and purpose and apply them to their sport.

In this chapter, you have been encouraged to obtain feedback. You should also provide feedback to other coaches. Based on your thinking and understanding and all the research that you have completed by reading through this book, you can offer valuable information to aid other coaches in their development. Coaches should serve as critical friends who can provide sound advice and at the same time identify the positive aspects of others' coaching.

Those who endeavour to be a thinking, proactive coach, and who take advantages of opportunities to improve their athletes' performance, enjoyment and lifestyle, will be the most successful coaches. These coaches will make a difference to sport and athlete development. Empowerment as a coaching approach provides athletes with a holistic learning environment in which they can learn about life and about sport.

No man really becomes a fool until he stops asking questions.

—*Charles Steinmetz, German-US electrical engineer*

Do not let what you cannot do interfere with what you can do.

—*John Wooden*

About the Contributing Authors

Robyn Jones

Dr Robyn Jones lectures in Sports Coaching at the University of Otago. His current research interests involve coach biographies and how coaches' values and philosophies shape their practice. His latest book, soon to be published by Longman, examines the practice of top-level coaches from the sociological perspectives of power, role and interaction. Having coached soccer in both Europe and the US, he is also currently the director of football for the Southern Federation (NZ).

Craig Lewis

Craig Lewis has been sport psychologist to a large number of New Zealand athletes over the past decade, including the 1994 Lillehammer Winter Olympic Games team. He was the inaugural director of the New Zealand Squash Institute, and has been sport psychologist to national champions, world champions and world record holders in both team and individual sports.

As a senior lecturer and acting head of the School of Sport at UNITEC Institute of Technology, Craig developed a number of sport programmes and qualifications, including the Bachelor of Sport Coaching degree. In his research, Craig has spent many years exploring and developing performance enhancement and athlete welfare initiatives. Craig is now the director of Sportlife New Zealand.

Rod Thorpe

Mr Rod Thorpe is the director of Sports Development at Loughborough University, United Kingdom. Rod qualified as a physical education teacher at the then Loughborough College of Education in 1964. After four years of teaching physical education with biology, Rod returned to Loughborough in 1968 to train teachers, and coached both rugby and tennis. In 1975 Rod studied for a research Masters degree in human biology at Loughborough University. His interest in psychology developed during his initial training but became more focused as a result of his experiences in teaching and coaching.

During his time at Loughborough, Rod has been part of a team developing sports technology—the application of sport science to sport, as well as innovative courses in physical education—leadership and coaching studies, reflecting on teaching and coaching. External work has included consultancies on sports leadership, coach education (coordinating one of the first National Coaching Foundation Centres), development of Top Sport programmes for children, and games teaching innovations both nationally and internationally.

Rod was Winston Churchill Fellow in 1992 and gained the International Olympic Committee Biennial Award in 1997.